**LIFE** AS I
**BLOW IT**

# SARAH COLONNA

VILLARD  NEW YORK

# LIFE AS I BLOW IT

## TALES OF LOVE, LIFE & SEX...
### NOT NECESSARILY IN THAT ORDER

A Villard Books Trade Paperback Original

Published in the United States by Villard Books, an imprint of The Random House Publishing Group, a division of Random House, Inc., New York.

VILLARD BOOKS and VILLARD & "V" CIRCLED Design are registered trademarks of Random House, Inc.

Library of Congress Cataloging-in-Publication Data
Colonna, Sarah.
Life as I blow it: tales of love, life & sex . . . not necessarily in that order / Sarah Colonna.
p.  cm.
ISBN 978-0-345-52837-7 (pbk.)
eBook ISBN 978-0-345-52838-4
1. Colonna, Sarah.   2. Women comedians—United States—Biography.
3. Television actors and actresses—United States—Biography.   I. Title.
PN2287.C5745A3 2012
792.702'8092—dc23         2011046763
[B]

Printed in the United States of America

www.ballantinebooks.com

3  4  5  6  7  8  9

Book design by Susan Turner
Title page photograph © Zan Passante

*To my mom. You never even blinked when I told you what I wanted to do with my life. You just believed in me. Thank you.*

*What I had in mind was spending the night
with a stranger who loves me.*

—DUDLEY MOORE, *Arthur* (1981)

# SLOPPY SARAH

*A Foreword by Chelsea Handler*

**S**arah Colonna believes that just because she dislodged her ass from Fayetteville, Arkansas, and moved all the way to Los Angeles, she no longer deserves to work at a fast-food chain called Chucky's. She is wrong. I don't know if there is a fast-food chain called Chucky's, but if there is, that's where she deserves to be.

I met Sarah at an improvisation class in the Valley when we were both twenty-one years old. We were magnetically drawn to each other because we both looked like we were in our mid-forties. The class was an embarrassment of riches and a testament that everything happens for a reason. Had I not looked to a sixty-year-old wannabe actor/comic for direction in weaving the name of a city and a profession, yelled out by another classmate, into a hilarious Southwest-level comedy bit, I would never have seen Sarah in her underwear. We have smoked cigarettes while wearing our Invisalign. Well, I was wearing mine, but she needs it.

Shortly after I met Sarah she inherited a cat from a male friend of hers who died. I felt bad that her friend had died, but I couldn't wrap my head around the idea of keeping someone else's cat. I knew she had to be from the South or the Midwest, and at the time both of those areas meshed together in my mind, so it really didn't matter. What mattered is that she kept that cat and it is still fucking alive.

We spent a lot of time together drinking excessively and waiting tables to pay for the former. She drove a smelly white Mustang with doors the size of chaise lounges and I drove a Toyota Echo. Both of those cars survived a lot of fast food, a lot of alcohol spilling, a lot of men, a lot of drive-bys, and a lot of fender benders that were not reported to the LAPD.

She paired that feculent Mustang with a horrifying haircut that I imagined you would find on a secretary from Omaha who worked full-time at a potato plant. I told her repeatedly to let her hair grow out, especially after I saw her license picture once, when we were both proving to each other how old we actually were. She had long blond hair when she was in college at the University of Arkansas and looked ten times better than the girl whose glassy eyes I was barely staring into. We were both drunk on her bed wondering why no one thought we were our actual age. At thirty-five we still have the same problem, so the idea that you grow into it is a complete lie.

We started doing stand-up together somewhere around 1997 and one of us would stop, and then start again, then one of us would stop; then we'd start again. The problem is we hung out so much that our stand-up was too much alike and people would get us confused all the time. All we both talked about was drinking and being broken up with by AM/PM mini-mart managers. We both kind of hated it, but knew there was really no other option for either one of us to get anywhere in life in the real world, and we were both too lazy to change our material. Sarah had more of an acting background. I had more of a bad-attitude background. Our biggest priority was fun and Sarah is probably the funniest person I know and I happen to know a lot of funny people. Unfortunately, none of them are the people I work with.

Cut to almost fifteen years and ten boyfriends later. She and I get to work together every day and I have forced her to share an office with one of the loudest Jewish eaters in the history of West Los Angeles. She is a huge part of *Chelsea Lately* and *After Lately* and is by far the most popular person in the office. Everyone loves Sarah. She is my favorite and she will be yours, too. If I write any more, this will start to sound like a eulogy. We've come a long way from using our debit cards at Del Taco. We both only eat organic Mexican now; excluding every other Thursday, when Chuy has us over for brunch.

# CONTENTS

SLOPPY SARAH:
A FOREWORD *by Chelsea Handler*       ix

WHERE DO I START?       3

HOW MANY POLACKS DOES IT TAKE
TO RUIN A MARRIAGE?       6

VOLUN-TEARS       19

HYMEN GO SEEK       39

FRIENDS WITHOUT BENEFITS       59

ALCOHOL IS FOR CLOSURES       80

CABO WOBBLE       100

TRUNDLE BEDS AND MASTURBATORS       115

HELL CAT       128

THE LIST                               140

BIKINI ROCK BOTTOM                     153

REALLY BAD HAIR DAY                    170

LIAR, LIAR, PANTS ON FIRE              178

DIRTY THIRTY                           193

THE CUSTOMER IS NEVER RIGHT            210

MOVE IT OR LOSE IT                     216

ALONE TIME                             229

CLOSING ARGUMENT                       234


ACKNOWLEDGMENTS                        237

# LIFE AS I BLOW IT

# WHERE DO I START?

I'm sitting alone in my apartment with a big glass of vodka next to me. I've filled it three times so far, and it's only 4 P.M. Whatever, it's Sunday.

I'm trying to figure out how to start this book. I've ended it, but I haven't started it. That's how I do a lot of things. I get to the end of a meal much faster than I should, like I've been given the last hamburger on earth and someone is about to rob me. I walk like I'm being chased. I tend to fuck first and ask questions later.

I'm thirty-six years old, but I don't feel like it. Some days I feel like I'm twenty-one, some days I feel like I'm pushing sixty. I work really hard and because of that I believe I should be able to play really hard. It's not easy to find a guy who can handle that. It's also not easy to find a guy who doesn't mind that at one point in my life, I slept with some-body named "Paul's friend."

To the naked eye, I'm completely responsible. I pay my bills not only on time, but early. I return emails and phone calls in a prompt manner. I won't go near an egg that is one second past its expiration date. I've always known what I want to do with my life professionally. But if you ask me what I want in my personal life, forget it.

I always wanted to get married, until it looked like someone might want to marry me. I was sure I didn't want kids, then for a couple of months I wanted kids, then a couple of months later I thought kids were horrible. I loved someone so much that I broke up with him because I didn't want to get hurt. Then when he proved he loved me back, I broke up with him again. I'm a fucking mess, but so are you. Most of us are. I don't just mean women. Men are a mess, too. We're all in this together.

We all have two very different personalities living inside us and sometimes those people are at war with each other. It's confusing to see what two completely different paths can offer you. My mom showed me that if you lived close to your family, you always had a birthday party. You also al-ways had a big Thanksgiving dinner, a big Christmas, an Easter egg hunt. Maybe those events became annoying, but you always knew you could rely on them. And you always had each other.

My dad showed me that if you went off on your own, you could have the career that you always wanted. Your family might change with each marriage and you might have to move around, feel alone for a while, and make new friends, but you'd always be climbing the ladder. Plus you could go on really nice vacations and stay in hotels with nice comfy robes that could be yours for the reasonable price of eighty-nine dollars.

I'm somewhere in the middle. I want both. Or I want it all. Or I only want part of both. I don't know. I just know that you don't always end up happy with what you thought would make you happy. You've probably been there a time or two yourself. You can't always want what you get.

## HOW MANY POLACKS DOES IT TAKE TO RUIN A MARRIAGE?

At the time of my parents' divorce, I was five years old and we were all living in Dallas. Lori came into our lives soon after. My mom's family was in Arkansas; she went there to look for a place for us to live so that she'd have a support system now that she was going to be a single mom. While she was gone, Lori stayed at our house in Dallas. She didn't seem to have many housekeeping skills, so I knew she wasn't a maid. Dad also suggested we didn't mention the amount of time Lori spent at our house to Mom, so I knew she wasn't a friendly gal pal. It all seemed to tie together to the time that Mom locked the dead bolt on the front door and then broke a broomstick in half and shoved it into the track of our back sliding-glass door. It was pretty late, so I asked her if she was scared that someone was going to break in. She just smiled and told me to go to bed. I woke up later when my dad tried to climb through a window and didn't fit. The next day, when I asked Dad why he got home after midnight he told me that he had worked late with Lori. This woman was around at really inconvenient times.

My older sister, Jennifer, and I were flower girls in Dad and Lori's wedding. Neither of us was too pumped up about the event, but we showed up and did our jobs. I didn't like weddings to begin with. I found them long and boring and it cut into the time I would normally spend playing "Charlie's Angels" with my sister. She was brunette, so she played Jaclyn Smith's character. I was awesome, so I played Cheryl Ladd's. The third Angel we just pretended was on vacation, because nobody we lived near wanted to be Kate Jackson. We had water guns and a telephone that didn't work so that we could report to "Charlie." Since we didn't have a brother, we considered ourselves very lucky that on the show nobody ever saw Charlie.

This wedding in particular really had me in a foul mood. I didn't like my new stepmom. She was annoying and made me eat some sort of salmon dish with the skin around it while she said things like "one day your mom and I will be the best of friends." I'd stare at her, try to count in my head all of the times my mom had called her a slut, spit my dinner into a napkin, and vow to hate her forever. She was also Polish, which made for lots of fun Polack jokes for Jennifer and me. Dad didn't find them amusing.

I tried to display my distaste for their union. I refused to eat cake at the reception, which at six was my way of saying "fuck you." The whole thing took place in my old backyard, where I used to live with my family in Dallas. Now it was my dad's house with a new woman who sucked and had a jacked-up nose. Lori made Jennifer and me wear brown floral skirts that went past our knees and off-white shirts that buttoned so high up the neck I thought I was going to choke to death. I went to my old room right after they exchanged vows, and on the way I mentioned to a dozen people that Lori's nostrils were a lot bigger than my mom's.

"If you'd like to see a photo comparison, I have one ready," I told one of my dad's co-workers. Nobody bit on the offer. Just as well, I needed to get to sleep. I was going back to Arkansas the next day and I needed all of my energy for wowing the flight attendants with my wit. "What has four legs and won't live longer than two years?" I'd ask them. One woman would guess a hamster; the other would be so stumped she wouldn't even have a guess. I'd smile proudly and deliver the punch line perfectly: "My dad's new marriage!"

I was hilarious. I made my first mental note to myself to become a comedian when I grew up.

By the way, their marriage lasted about two years. The day Dad asked me, "How do you get a one-armed Polack out of a tree?" I knew it was over.

When they separated, Lori sent letters to my sister and me asking if we could stay in touch and still be friends. I guess she didn't realize we weren't friends when she and Dad *were* married. I thought I had made it obvious that I never liked her. I made a mental note to make that more clear to people in the future.

While it only took my dad a handful of months to remarry, my mom was not interested in dating. She was a single mom living in Fayetteville, Arkansas. She was too busy working and raising us to care about finding a man. She probably also hated men for a while, but I wasn't old enough to figure that out yet.

After the divorce, her first job was at a school cafeteria. She refused to work at our school, because she thought we'd be embarrassed. I told her of course I wouldn't be embarrassed that my mom was a lunch lady, then ran to my room and thanked God that she had chosen a different school. I also apologized to Him for lying to her, but it seemed like a necessary one.

After a bit of prodding from some friends, Mom decided to join a singles' group. In my mind it wasn't a good idea. I don't know if they even have those anymore; I think online dating has replaced them. Later on in the book, you'll find out why I think online dating sucks ass. Stick with me here, it's a really humiliating story. I promise.

I pictured my mom's singles' group taking place in one of those weird banquet rooms at a hotel. There's a long table set up in front covered with name tags. Mom walks up and finds hers: HELLO, MY NAME IS CHERYL. She pins it to her red mock turtleneck, smoothes out her Lands' End slacks, and nervously walks into the room. She immediately heads for the refreshment table and scans the contents—coffee and donuts—then fixes herself a cup of decaf; she doesn't want to get too wound up. She notices a couple of people looking at her. *Oh, good, people are already noticing me.* She starts to relax, then finds their gazes to be strange. It feels like they are smirking, laughing. *Oh, no,* she thinks to herself. *They must all know that my husband left me and that he is already remarried. I must smell like a victim.* She starts thinking that this was a terrible idea. *Why did I let anybody talk me into this? What the hell am I doing here?* she wonders. She starts to feel dizzy. She looks around frantically for the ladies' room. She walks briskly to the restroom; she just needs a minute to compose herself. She runs in and finds the bathroom empty. *Thank God, a minute alone.* She walks to the sink and turns on the faucet. She runs cold water over her hands and then onto her face. As she rises from the sink she opens her eyes to look at herself in the mirror. Horror washes over her. She forgot to take off her hair net after work. She rips it off, throws it in the trash, and leaves the hotel. *Maybe next time,* she decides as she makes her way to her car.

At least that's what I always imagined it was like. I watch a lot of Lifetime movies.

At some point she found her groove in the group. She had a few dates with a couple of different people. Mom had become friends with some of the other women, and one of them tipped her off to someone who could babysit us while she went out. I don't remember the babysitter's name. I just know I called her "Penny," which was short for *Pentecostal,* because, well, she was Pentecostal. I didn't really know what that was at the time. My mom was Methodist and my dad was busy. I went to church from time to time with Mom but there wasn't much to our religion. Everybody was nice and it didn't seem like there were a ton of rules. The preacher did a sermon, a couple of hymns were sung, someone passed around the offering tray, and we were out. Pretty basic. That was not the case with Penny. She took her religion very, very seriously. She refused to cut her hair; I think she thought it was a direct line to God. It was long and stringy and almost touched the ground, kind of like Crystal Gayle but without the hit records. From what I could tell, her religion didn't like skin, because she wore long, straight skirts and shirts that buttoned all the way up to her chin. Her outfits kind of reminded me of what I had to wear when Dad married Lori.

When I first met Penny I asked Mom if she was Amish, but Mom told me never to ask Penny that to her face. So the next time I saw her, I asked. She told me that she was not Amish, but thanked me for the interest in her life.

"I'm Pentecostal," she continued. "Would you like me to explain to you what my religion is?"

"Maybe next time. I'm pretty wiped," I lied. God immediately got me back because now I had committed to going to bed at 7 P.M.

One night Mom had a date on a Wednesday. That was Penny's church night, so she was never available to sit for us. Mom called her anyway, thinking maybe just this one time she'd need the money and skip church. Obviously Mom had never really paid any attention to Penny because she would *never* miss church. Unfortunately for me, my previous inquiry into Penny's religion had stuck in her mind. She told Mom that she would gladly watch Jennifer and me. She'd just take us to church with her. I couldn't believe I had to go to church on a Wednesday night. This seemed unfair.

"We have to go to church so that you can go on a date!" I yelled in as high a pitch as I could get my voice to. It doesn't go that high. I'm often confused for a man on the phone.

"That's right," my mom said. Her newfound confidence was getting annoying.

"Well, maybe I don't want to go. Maybe I'll go live with Dad."

"Okay, say hi to Lori for me."

*Shit. Mom is getting good.*

Penny's church was nothing like I had imagined. When we walked in, I began to wonder how all these people had the time to go shopping together. Every single person was dressed the same. Long skirts, button-up shirts, and the same color pants on the men. There was hair everywhere. Some wore it in buns, others let it drag on the floor. I figured they must all have pretty decent jobs if they were able to afford the shampoo it requires for the upkeep.

We filed into a pew and waited for things to start. I was already antsy—like I was alone in a foreign country and I didn't speak the language. Things started off kind of normal. The preacher started talking, reading, talking. It was all par for the course. Just when I thought that it was going to be no big deal, things started to turn. The preacher asked people to come forward if they needed to be "saved" or if they wanted to renew their vow to God. Droves of people started making their way down the aisle. Suddenly they were crying, yelling, singing. Some people didn't even make it to the front of the church. They just fell on their knees and started wailing. Their hands were in the air, reaching up to God. But they were mostly just flailing. My sister and I looked at each other in a mixture of horror, confusion, and humor. *What is going on?* I looked up to Penny thinking maybe she'd be ready to bail since clearly all of her church buddies had gone insane, but she just stared straight ahead and nodded. At one point I noticed a single tear run down her cheek. That was it—she had lost her mind. I gripped the pew and braced myself. I knew in my heart that the whole place was about to burst into flames, or I was about to be entered into a cult and never heard from again.

"Mom better at least be getting laid for this," Jennifer whispered to me.

"EEW! Don't say that!" I was horrified. For many years I was a big prude compared to my sister. That changed around the time I developed a taste for Wild Turkey.

Eventually things died down. The service came to an end and as far as I could tell nobody had passed away during all the drama. Penny led my sister and me out to her car, where the two of us waited patiently for an explanation. I had it all figured out: Outside of her appearance, Penny seemed pretty normal when she was watching us. There was no way that she brought us to this circus knowing that her friends were going to lose their shit. Obviously she couldn't say anything in the church; they probably knew where she lived. She was just going through the motions, then when she got us in the car, she'd tell us that she'd never seen anything like that in her life and that she was so sorry that everyone at her church got possessed at the same time, especially on the night we had to go with her. "What a bunch of freaks!" she'd say, laughing.

Penny turned the engine on and looked at us in the rearview mirror. She gave us a knowing smile and asked, "Who wants ice cream?"

That night I waited up for my mom. I was usually in bed early; the anxious adult me hadn't crept in yet to convince myself that six hours of sleep was plenty. As a kid I knew I needed my brain rest so that I could get straight A's, go to college, and make a bunch of money so that I could get out of this town.

"What are you still doing up?" Mom asked.

"Couldn't sleep. How was your night?"

"It was all right. How was yours?" she replied.

"Penny and the people who go to her church are ba-nanas. You sent us to an insane asylum. If you ever have a date on a Wednesday night again, don't. Night!"

With that I went off to bed.

Mom's singles' group seemed to be restoring some of her self-confidence and she decided she no longer wanted to work at a cafeteria. She started looking for a new job and quickly found one at a funeral home, where she became a secretary. She didn't have to touch dead bodies, but it was still creepy. She would come home and make dinner and talk about how "busy" it was, which just meant that lots of people had died. My sister and I were not really into her work talk, and I think she took offense at it. I was really proud of her for getting a good job, and I was really glad she felt more security. But sorry—I was trying to eat.

For a while when we were living in Fayetteville we lived next door to two guys who were close in age to my sister and me. They became our best friends, and one had the honor of my first tongue kiss. His name was Kevin and I liked him so much that I named my first goldfish after him. He was super cute and he told funny stories. The neighbor, not the goldfish. The goldfish didn't say much. I had found my true love, and I was only eight.

Kevin was really popular in school. He pretty much ran our elementary homeroom and all the girls liked him. I counted myself lucky to have tied down such a free spirit. It also worked out well that we were neighbors. He walked me home—well, his house was first, so he'd stop there, and I'd walk the next four houses alone. It was okay, though. My expectations were pretty low to begin with, so it seemed like he was doing a great job as my first boyfriend.

Although my love life was in great shape, there still weren't any prospects panning out for my mom from the singles' group. I felt kind of bad that I was eight years old and in love while my thirty-three-year-old mom was struggling to want to go on a second date.

During one of the busy afternoons at my mom's work, a guy who made the flower deliveries for the funeral home struck up a conversation with her. He found her charming and sweet and wondered if she was available. She looked at the ring on his hand then shot him a disapproving look.

"No, not for me," he said with a laugh. "My wife would kill me. But you should meet my friend Eric."

When my mom met Eric, I was skeptical. Things were going smoothly. Jennifer and I had settled in as "latchkey kids" and Mom had stopped talking about dead bodies during supper. I wasn't sure I wanted someone else in the mix. But he won me over fairly quickly; he was pretty easy to like. He used words like *reckon* and *plumb* (as in: "That house is plumb out in the middle of nowhere" and "I reckon we need to get some gas"). I'm still not sure what those words mean, but at the same time I am. No matter what was in his vocabulary, I could tell he was incredibly smart. He spewed out historical and political facts, but for a living he worked at Tyson Foods. He also knew a lot about geography, and I still can't read a map. So I was impressed, *and* I had someone to help me with my homework.

My mom had a pretty bad overbite, and since she was falling in love she decided to have it fixed. That decision resulted in her mouth being wired shut for about six weeks, which was awesome. My mom really likes to talk, so this was the equivalent of taking brunch away from a gay man.

The only word she could say clearly was *shit,* and she had to eat all her food through a straw. She'd make Jennifer and me nice dinners, then suck sadly on a green shake.

The best part of her not being able to talk was that she couldn't tell us to do chores. She'd try, but we'd just say we couldn't understand her and then erupt in giggles. The use of the word *shit* would then start flowing, I think preceded by *you little* but I couldn't quite make it out. Eric was a real trouper through that whole thing. I think he just enjoyed the quiet.

When they decided to get married, it was announced that we'd have to move. We were living in Fayetteville and they wanted to buy a house together a few miles away in the small town of Farmington. Moving to Farmington meant we had to change schools.

My head exploded. *What the hell are they thinking?* My relationship with Kevin was really starting to flourish. Just the week before, he had apologized for not taking me to the Valentine's Day dance. He finally agreed that it was weird that I went alone and that when I got there he ignored me. He was really sorry! How could I move away and go to a new school when we'd just worked through our first huge fight and were going to be stronger than ever? I was really starting to make some headway here, and for once I'd stuck up for myself. I made him promise not to ignore me in public anymore. I even told him that if he did it one more time I wouldn't allow him to ever walk me halfway home from school again.

Shortly after I got the news that my life was being dismantled, I walked up to Kevin's house to tell him. I was envisioning his tears and heartache; it would be very dramatic. When I got close to his yard, I noticed that Kevin and his brother were throwing something around like a football, so I assumed it was a football. As I got closer I stopped in my tracks. The football was making a lot of noise. It was meowing. The football was a cat.

I ran to him in tears and demanded that he stop throwing the cat. He laughed and continued to torture the defenseless animal. I managed to step in the middle, which only made me become part of an involuntary game of keep-away. I'm not sure keep-away is ever voluntary; I just know that it's really frustrating. After a while I managed to get the cat away and I ran with him in my arms to my house while shouting back over my shoulder that I was going to call the ASPCA on him. I was really impressed with myself for knowing what the ASPCA was. Eric had told me.

I ran home and tearfully told my mother the story. She looked at me with sad eyes and patted me on the head for saving the cat from those assholes. She didn't say anything, not because she was speechless but because her mouth was still wired shut. We fed the cat some mystery meat dish that my mother had made the night before—she's got a lot of great qualities, but cooking is not one of them, though many say the same about me—then dialed the number on his collar and returned him to his owners, who promised they would never use him as a football.

When I got to my room I noticed that Kevin, my goldfish, was floating at the top of his bowl. He was dead, and now to me so was the other Kevin. It all came full circle. I buried the goldfish in a little box and dramatically said goodbye to Kevin my first boyfriend and to Kevin the Goldfish. The next day I found out through Jennifer's taunting that I could have just flushed the fish, which pissed me off further at Kevin the boyfriend for once again wasting my time, since I blamed him for the death of my beloved fish. Even though he had nothing to do with it.

I gave up on my fight to stay in Fayetteville at Happy Hollow Elementary. Since I had broken it off with Kevin, I had little reason to want to stay in that school district. Now I was the one ignoring him and it was really awkward for everyone in our homeroom. I was ready for a change. I had so many other things I wanted to do, places I wanted to see, and relationships I wanted to develop. It's like when you're in your thirties and you realize you haven't done half of the things you always said you'd do . . . but you're eight.

# VOLUN-TEARS

I currently live in Los Angeles. I work on a late-night talk show and I do stand-up several weekends out of the year. I don't have kids and thus far the only person I've felt really comfortable living with is myself. And sometimes I'm not a big fan of her, either.

I live what some might consider to be a pretty great life. Others probably think that it's selfish, or that I'm missing something. It's tough for me to say who is right and who is wrong. Because where I come from and where I am now are two very different places.

In Los Angeles, I often go to the Coffee Bean & Tea Leaf with my friend Jackie at noon on Saturdays because we know that the firefighters from Station 19 are going to be there at that time for a coffee fix. They're fun to look at. In Farmington, Arkansas, firefighters look different. They look like my family. Mostly because they *are* my family.

If your mother's entire family was deeply involved in a volunteer fire department, you probably would have moved away from Arkansas, too. At one point my grandmother, Phyllis, was the fire chief, and she wasn't even a lesbian. She just liked being in charge. Everyone else in my family, besides me, was a volunteer firefighter. It's something they're all very proud of. As a teenager who just wanted to get felt up, I found it all pretty annoying. As a semi-mature adult, I'm now proud to say my family saves lives. So maybe stop judging me now and let's try and get along for the rest of the book.

Most of the other members of the Wedington Volunteer Fire Department (the name Farmington was already taken by the town's professional fire department; we had to settle for naming ours after a street) served on the mysterious "board." They had monthly meetings and if someone didn't show up, my mom sure talked shit about them. I knew that being a volunteer meant you also had to have a real job, so I would suggest to her that some people were probably just too tired to make it to the meetings after a long day at work. My mom would argue back that those people probably should not volunteer to fight fires, then.

"Would you want to depend on someone who can't even show up for a monthly meeting to save your house if it was burning down?" she'd ask me.

"I guess not."

The whole thing was pretty cutthroat, and way too much of a commitment for me.

There were several side projects that the fire department had going in order to keep afloat, one being the fire department cookbook. As we got older, my sister, Jennifer, began to contribute recipes. I did not. Like I said, I've never been much of a cook. I cook for myself sometimes, but it doesn't taste very good. It actually tastes pretty awful. I prefer to dine out. My family likes to make fun of me, indicating that being able to cook is part of what makes a woman a woman. I disagree. Getting my period makes me a woman. Cooking just makes me bored.

Most members would submit a recipe, and all these fabulous recipes were bound together in a flimsy little booklet with a yellow cover. I think they sold them for ten dollars, which was a huge rip-off. I can't imagine how many people got the book home and realized that "Virginia's Secret Creamy Mac and Cheese" was just fucking mac-and-cheese. I mean, the recipe actually included buying a box of Kraft macaroni and cheese, then following instructions. That seemed like cheating to me.

My mother contributed her famous original recipe for "Kung Fu Pasta." It was something I ate a lot growing up, and I'm not going to lie . . . it is delicious. It's the one thing she made really well. It consists of spaghetti noodles, diced carrots, diced pork chop, and something green. The "Kung Fu" part came from the fact that she topped it off with soy sauce. It wasn't until I was in my twenties that it dawned on me the name of that pasta might be slightly offensive to people, like people who do kung fu.

There are some responsibilities while living under your parents' roof that you just can't get out of. For me, one of those things was the fire department's pancake breakfast. It was held at 6 A.M. a few Saturdays a year. My mom keeps telling me now that it was only once a year, but I know she's lying to try to make my childhood sound more fun.

When the breakfast rolled around, I'd be forced to get out of bed, put on a bright yellow T-shirt that said WEDING-TON VOLUNTEERS that was three sizes too big, and serve pancakes and sausage to everyone I knew. The only other thing I did as humiliating was work at Hardee's, but at least that paid.

My best friend in high school was Lindsay. She played basketball and I was on drill team. We liked to do the same things, like drink Busch Light and smoke Marlboro 100's. After first seeing the movie *Thelma & Louise,* she and I started drinking Wild Turkey. Susan Sarandon and Geena Davis drank it while on the run from the cops for a crime they really shouldn't have been in trouble for, and they seemed to enjoy it. Wild Turkey is 101 proof, which means its alcohol content is over 50 percent, which was more than triple my age when I developed a taste for it. I liked to chase it with Coke, then when I'd run out of Coke I'd drink it straight—just like Thelma and Louise did.

Discovering bourbon at fifteen didn't do much to help my mood when I had to show up, work pancake duty, and deal with the annoying crowd. At the time I believed that the only people who *should* wake up that early to stand in line for food that's made in mass quantities were homeless people. But I wasn't dealing with people in need. I was just dealing with people who were overweight, cheap, or both. And I was usually hungover.

But before all that, it took me a while to fall in love again. I was still healing from having been duped by a man who was abusive to animals and I wasn't about to let myself fall for another liar. Men obviously pulled you in with their charm and good looks, then one day, wham! You find out that it's all been a lie and there you are on *Maury Povich* trying to warn other women of the signs that their man might be leading a double life. This is exactly what my mother must have felt like when my father left. I was really beginning to understand marriage, and I didn't like what I saw.

Then I met Ricky Walden. We were in seventh grade together. He had a rattail haircut and he knew how to break-dance. Clearly he was *really* popular. We all gathered around him at recess while he spun around on his back and hit fake home runs with his fake baseball bat. He was amazing. I was attracted to bad boys. It wasn't my fault.

I let Ricky finger me on a field trip. We were on the bus and it was dark. We had a blanket over us and I decided to let him go for it. Thus far the only person that had touched my vagina was me, so it was a big event to let him do so. Looking back, I can't believe the teachers let us cover up with a giant blanket, but maybe they noticed I was a little uptight for a seventh grader and figured I could use the release. I couldn't wait to tell my best friend, Lindsay, the next day at school. *She's going to die! I got fingered!* This was huge.

The next day I didn't have to tell anybody—everybody already knew. Apparently Ricky had taken the time out of his busy break-dancing schedule to let everyone know what he and I had done on the bus. *What a nightmare.* I had really only planned on telling Lindsay. I was a very private person, and I was terrified of being known as a slut before I was in high school.

Once I found out that everyone knew, Lindsay and I had an emergency meeting in the bathroom. I cried hysterically. She reminded me that almost everybody else had already been fingered, except the Baptists. She was pretty sure they had, too, but that they were less honest about it. The pow-wow lifted my spirits and I went through the rest of the day feeling pretty good, until I walked out to catch the bus and saw Ricky letting Jimmy Thompson smell his fingers. I waited until he saw me, then I dramatically raised my middle finger and stormed off. Giving him the finger felt like poetic justice.

I heard a lot of oohs and aahs and was pretty proud of myself for once again telling a guy what was up. I went home and took the yellow sweatshirt with teddy bears on it that I had worn the night Ricky and I had our moment, and threw it in the trash. As a side note, Jimmy Thompson used to pee in his sweats. Glass house, throwing stones—that whole thing.

I'm a fan of sleep, and now I don't get enough of it. I can't even comprehend when someone tells me they have to get their "eight hours in" or else they can't function. I shoot for seven, usually get six, and manage to function. I'm not always in a great mood, but I function. I might have gotten the sleep problem from my dad. He tends to stay up really late and yet wake up early. I developed that same habit when I was bartending, and at thirty-six it seems to just be my pattern. As a teenager my sleep would often be interrupted by the scanner. That's the really annoying thing that goes off to alert volunteers that there's a fire. It sat on a long buffet in our dining room. It was always on.

That scanner was an asshole. I swear there isn't anything more terrifying than being woken up at 3 A.M. to the crackling voice of whoever got the shitty late-night shift, which was usually whoever didn't show up for the board meeting that month. My heart would race as I'd hear the voice screaming "ATTENTION WEDINGTON VOLUN-

TEERS, WE GOT A BRUSH FIRE ON OL' MILLS ROAD!"
It's a terrible way to be woken up, and it happened all of the
time.

When I'd get home from school and was alone, I would
sometimes turn the scanner off in an attempt at some peace
and quiet. I needed to watch *General Hospital,* and I didn't
need any interruptions. It worked out great for me, but not
so great for my stepdad, Eric. I had gotten so wrapped up in
the Quartermaines' drama one time that I had failed to turn
the volume back up on the scanner. There was a huge fire
and the only person from our family who didn't show up
was Eric. They all teased him the next day: "Sounds like
someone had too much pie for dessert and couldn't get out
of the recliner!" They were relentless.

I felt terrible. Eric was the newest member of the family
and he wanted them all to know he took the fire department
seriously. I didn't feel bad enough to tell the whole family
that it was my fault, though. Grandma would have killed me
if she'd known I'd turned off the scanner to watch a soap
opera.

I tried to apologize to Eric. "I'm really sorry you missed
the fire at the Millers' house, but Robin Scorpio's boyfriend
Stone grew up in the streets. He got sick and was afraid he
had HIV. Today was when they gave the results."

He just walked away and went to bed.

"His test came back positive if you care! I hope they find
a cure soon! Eric?"

This is the same man who offered to get a second job just
to make sure I could go to college, so you'd think I could
have come clean about whose fault it was, but I was a teenager and I found the whole thing really ridiculous. What
was the point of volunteering? There were firefighters who

got paid, after all. Let them risk their lives and let's stay home and enjoy Kung Fu Pasta like a normal family.

My family also gathered yearly to chop wood for the winter. It wasn't until I moved to California that I learned about gas fireplaces. It would have been pretty fucking nice to have had one of those growing up. I could've gotten a lot more sleep during that one Saturday in the winter and I never would have had to know what size I wore in wood-chopping gloves. My mom's side of the family obviously has a thing for fire. Maybe I shouldn't complain about something I only had to do once a year, but I was a teenager. I didn't think I should be out in the woods unless I was drinking bourbon or having teenage sex. I really needed to get out of this situation. My dad never did any manual labor, so I decided to look further into that.

Dad lived in sunny California. Visiting him in the summer was always a win-win. That was back when kids on a plane were treated like they were special. They'd let me and Jennifer, who is three years older than me, see the cockpit before takeoff and give us a pin shaped like wings. Maybe that was because my mom warned them that every time that I flew I threw up. That didn't stop until I was in college, by the way.

The flight attendants always told Jennifer and me that we were honorary co-pilots. They never took me up on my offer to actually help out when it was time for takeoff, but I was pretty sure they respected me as their peer. It always made me feel so cool. Nobody else I went to school with had that kind of experience. Sure, their families were still together, but we were racking up airline miles. And none of them knew about my compulsive vomiting. *Colonna Sisters 1, Everybody Else 0.*

My dad was a newspaper sports editor. When my parents first split up, he was working for the *Dallas Morning News*. Then while I was in about the fifth grade, he got a promotion and moved to California to work at the *Orange County Register*. By the time I was in high school he had moved on to the *Los Angeles Times*. He was always moving up and his job seemed to pay well because he had a pool that was not above the ground.

I know that lots of kids from divorced families hate leaving their friends for the summer, but I wasn't one of those kids. I enjoyed spinning tales of California and the ocean and all of the movie stars' houses that I'd seen on the "Map of the Stars' Homes" tour. Sometimes all you'd see was a bunch of trees and the tour guide would just assure you that Brad Pitt's house was on the other side, which is probably why my dad would lecture me that it was a rip-off. I didn't really care. I was fine being lied to as long as I got a relaxing trolley ride out of it. Plus I had already decided that one day I was going to be a famous actress. I needed to familiarize myself with the neighborhood. When I did finally move to Hollywood, I couldn't afford to live in the places that they showed me on that tour. I suffered in a tiny one-bedroom with no air-conditioning. It was behind Grauman's Chinese Theatre, which is a huge tourist trap. I could barely get out of my driveway without having to brake for a guy in a worn-out Spider-Man costume who was on his way to make money by disappointing children with his dirty tights and frail figure. Finally one day I decided that I deserved better. So for now I rent a decent condo in what's known as "the Valley." And I have central air.

One summer I took my picture with a cardboard cutout of Patrick Swayze for ten dollars across from Grauman's. It was so worth the money; I was sure that all of the morons I went to high school with would believe I had actually met Patrick Swayze. Unfortunately only one person bought my story. She was the same girl who thought that if you took a bath after sex you wouldn't get pregnant. She now has five kids. I never got to meet Patrick Swayze.

There weren't many rules at my dad's. From what I could gather, money equaled fun. Not that we were poor and struggling back home; my mom and Eric made enough money and took great care of us. But whatever my dad had going on certainly afforded him a lot more luxuries than I was used to. You know, things that don't matter but are fantastic to have. My mom was also a neat freak and didn't really understand sleeping in. At Dad's nobody ever woke me up early on a Saturday morning with a vacuum, and the only kind of pancake breakfasts I ever attended with him were at the International House of Pancakes. I actually don't remember ever seeing him do any sort of housework. His place was always really clean so someone must have done it. My mom would scoff at this notion.

"Oh he's big-time now. He probably has a maid. But at least I don't have to be his maid anymore," she'd remind me as she stood on my bed dusting my ceiling fan and explaining to me the dust wouldn't be falling on my head if I'd just get the fuck up. That was usually around 7:45 A.M. She was scheduled to vacuum at eight and everyone knows you always dust before you vacuum.

"Maybe you should get a maid," I told her no less than a million times.

"Never."

My mom now has a housekeeper. In Arkansas you can get one once every couple of weeks for the reasonable price of $35.99. I'm glad she figured out that she deserves to relax after work. But she still cleans up on the day the woman is supposed to come so that the housekeeper doesn't see her house dirty. I think she has a problem.

Since Farmington *was* such a small town everybody knew everybody. My mom's brothers and their wives lived within a couple of miles from us. So did my grandparents and their friends. We were a tight-knit group. My entire life there, every birthday was celebrated with a gathering. It still is. I get cakes in my thirties just like I did when I was a kid; the only difference is now they aren't shaped like a bunny rabbit with licorice for the whiskers. For every single member of the family's birthday, we all got together and there was pizza and cake and little to no booze. My mom's side of the family was a lot different than my dad's. When I was visiting my dad, parties were fun. When I was home at my mom's, parties were tame. The loveliness of it all escaped me and I just wanted to know when it would be over so I could go in my room and talk on the phone and listen to Def Leppard. The most exciting part of any gathering was when a fire would erupt and I'd watch every person in the house scatter. I'd then help myself to the remainder of the pizza and ponder who would be there for me if that house went up in flames.

Dad's family was different. The only person I was close to on his side of our family was his mom. She was wonderful. She'd take the Greyhound all the way from California to visit my sister and me in Arkansas. She lived alone and was a big drinker. I think at some point she drank rubbing alcohol, so she might have been more than just a drinker. She used to send me pictures of herself that she took with a Polaroid. She'd use the handle of a flyswatter to push the button on the camera, so every photo she sent had this long white handle stemming from her arm. It was a reminder to me that she lived alone. Her husband was remarried and she was not, but she was always smiling. Maybe it was the vodka, but all I knew was that she looked happy.

When Dad wasn't married, he usually had a girlfriend, sometimes two. I really didn't want to have to hang out with these women. It seemed like such a waste to buddy up with someone who obviously had no idea what she was up against. The odds of things working out for the two of them were never in her favor. I have to give it to Dad, though—he always tried. You could tell he really loved these people, or at least thought he did. He was probably just in love with the idea of being in love, but at that age I hadn't yet been to therapy, so I couldn't offer him that sort of insight. He's now been happily married for fifteen years to a wonderful woman, by the way. I guess sometimes it just takes a few tries to find your perfect match. And he tried four times.

One time when Jennifer and I went to visit him in California he had a new girlfriend named Candy. She was exactly what you'd expect you'd get from a woman with that name. Blond, big boobs, stupid. We hadn't met her yet, so Dad decided to bring her with him to pick us up at the airport. I was pretty annoyed: I hadn't seen him in a year and now I had to put up with this disaster all the way to his house. She tried to talk to me, so I pretended to fall asleep and left my sister to maintain the conversation. When we got to Dad's house I pretended to wake up and we got our bags and went inside. Dad then went back out to the car with Candy.

"I'm going to take her home. I'll be back in a little bit."

"What? We just got here!" I whined.

"I'll be right back!" With that he and Candy drove off into the night.

I couldn't understand why he didn't just drop her off before we got home. Wouldn't that have made more sense than leaving us there by ourselves? Jennifer explained that he probably wanted to have sex with her and it would be easier at her place.

"Gross! Her boobs are gross. I hate her."

"Me too," Jennifer decided. "By the way, nice fake sleeping in the car. Way to leave me stuck talking to Candy Cane."

"Sorry, I'm just a really good actress."

The rest of the summer we didn't see much of Candy. She went out to dinner with us one night the week that we arrived, and I could see that Dad was already losing interest in her. Maybe her stupidity was only fun for a few days? I hoped that was the case, but I didn't want to bring it up. I figured I'd count her absence as a blessing and leave it at that. It would have been too embarrassing to have a stepmom named Candy.

Regardless of who my dad was dating or married to when I came to visit, I got to do cool shit and meet interesting people. Since he was in sports, I was able to meet a handful of famous athletes, although I didn't know who most of them were. Most of my sports interest was in Friday night football at my school, and my halftime dance with the drill team. Regardless, I'd go home and brag to the guys in my class that I got to meet Jack Youngblood, whoever that was. They were impressed. Mission accomplished.

The only thing I really paid attention to in the professional sports world was baseball. I always liked going to Angels' games with my dad in the summer. That was when

they were the California Angels, before they were the Anaheim Angels, and way before they became the Los Angeles
Angels of Anaheim. Don't get me started.

We usually had to watch the game from a press suite,
which meant tons of free food and sneaking little bottles of
booze when nobody was looking. I'd take my Coke that I
had spiked with bourbon out to one of the seats and watch
the game from there with the rest of the loyal fans. What
were these press people doing inside chatting when they
could be outside taking in the game and all of the players'
nice asses? My teenage hormones really loved baseball.

Those summers I sat in the stands and dreamed of being
a baseball wife. Sure, I heard stories about the kind of life
that those people lived. Baseball wives put on a smile and
clapped in the stands, but inside they were sad. Their hus-
bands were always gone. They got tired of being alone so
they'd try to go to all of the games, including away games.
Then they'd get tired of being on the road. They'd go back
home but then they'd hear heartbreaking rumors about who
was having an affair with whom so they'd drink chardonnay
and take on lovers to hide the pain. I thought it sounded
awesome. Still do. I really need to stop watching Lifetime.

Unfortunately I never met any guys when I was visiting
Dad. I had a few girlfriends in California, but most were
daughters of people who Dad worked with. This one girl,
Stephanie, was really impressive to me. She was a full-on
California girl. She grew up there and she had the tan to
prove it. I'm sure now she has the sun damage and wrinkles
to prove it, but I bet she doesn't care. She also liked to
smoke, which piqued my interest. We spent several afternoons together; we usually had her mom or my dad drop us

off at the mall. We'd walk around for a while, taking the occasional smoke break. She told me stories of going to junior high in California. She said that people had parties at their parents' houses and took a bunch of Dramamine. Apparently the right amount of it made you hallucinate. I told her I had taken "my fair share" of Dramamine and she seemed impressed. I didn't bother to explain that it was never more than two and it was because of the in-flight vomiting.

Stephanie had an older sister, Brie. She was Jennifer's age and they were friends. I don't know what they did during their hang-out time together, but I think it was more impressive than looking for tank tops at Express and smoking. At one point my sister was out with Brie and she met a guy. He was in the army or something. I didn't know exactly what he did, I just knew he had a short haircut and talked about tough training. Jennifer decided that she was in love with him. She spoke tragically of the upcoming end to the summer and how she'd have to go back to Arkansas and leave her true love in California. She told me that "Right Here Waiting" by Richard Marx was their song.

*"Oceans apart, day after day, and I slowly go insane . . ."* Jennifer would recite the words of the song to me while she cried about leaving him. I felt bad for her, but I was more interested in what ocean she thought separated California and Arkansas. I guessed that Eric wasn't helping her with geography.

When we returned home after the summer, Jennifer announced to Mom that she was in love, that her new boyfriend was coming to visit for a week, and that he'd be staying with us. His name was Greg and he was going to be Mom's

son-in-law when Jennifer turned eighteen, so she might as
well welcome him with open arms. My mom stared at her
for a long time, then simply said, "Fine."

"Really?" Jennifer asked.

"Really?" I also asked.

"Really," Mom said. "Oh, just one thing. He's not staying in the house. He can sleep in the camper."

The camper was in our driveway. Greg was going to
have to fly to Arkansas and camp in our driveway if he
wanted to see Jennifer. Sure, we had a decent camper, complete with a TV and a table that converted to a bed, but it
certainly wasn't a place you wanted to make company sleep.
It *definitely* wasn't the place you wanted your future husband to have to sleep the first time he visited you.

Greg sucked it up and came to stay with us. He slept in
his designated area outside and didn't seem to mind too
much. He thought it was a pretty nice trailer.

"Do you guys use it often?" he inquired.

"We use it a lot when it's nice out," I explained. "During
the winter it just sits there, but Mom hides our Christmas
presents in it. Let me know if you see a pair of Z. Cavariccis
in any of the cabinets. I better get them this year."

After Greg went back to California, Jennifer stopped
talking about him and eventually she never brought him up
again. Sometimes when people show you that they really
care about you, you don't care about them anymore. Later
on in life, I'd find out that I could relate.

A couple of broken engagements and three or so years
after Lori, my dad got married again. Her name was Carol,
and she was kind of a bitch.

She worked at a rival newspaper, so she and Dad would
drink coffee in the morning and talk about what was wrong

with each other's paper. They had kind of a love-hate relationship, mostly consisting of hate. There was one thing I liked about Carol and that was that she let me drink wine. I think she was just doing what she could to get through our summer visits. It was half-water/half-wine, but it was better than nothing. She always let Jennifer and me have it with dinner, under the expectation that we wouldn't go home and tell our mom that her twelve- and fifteen-year-old daughters were allowed to drink when we went to California. That wasn't going to be a problem. We certainly weren't going to open our mouths and ruin our fun.

I remember once she took me shopping with her so that she could buy an outfit for some sort of opening of some sort of library. She purchased a $2,000 silk suit and some shoes that ran about $450. My feelings were mixed with shock and awe. Spending that kind of money on one outfit would have sent my mother to a mental institution. I was sure she'd be in a ton of trouble when she got home, and I was kind of looking forward to watching Dad yell at her, especially since she had denied me a really cute pair of jeans.

When we got back, I noticed she didn't mention it to him. He just asked if she found what she needed, she said that she had, and that was the end of that. I later let the price of her outfit slip out on purpose, but Dad seemed unfazed. "It's her money," he said flatly. He had no idea how much that one statement would impact me forever. It wasn't "their money," it was "her money." She could do whatever she wanted to do because she made her own money. *Good to know.*

I then became even more pissed that she didn't spring for the sixty-dollar jeans I wanted, and decided to expect some pretty good shit for Christmas from her that year.

Halfway through my senior year of high school my dad took my sister and me on a cruise with him and Carol. We were both pretty excited. This was when I thought cruises were cool, before I discovered that vacationing with hundreds of people and doing group aerobics on a deck was pretty humiliating.

The cruise was going to Mexico, and up to that point the only part of Mexico we'd seen was Tijuana, which was only good for stocking up on cheap dolls and maracas to show off back home. We managed to have a lot of fun on the ship, the highlight of the cruise being the Rod Stewart impersonator. He ran around in a Speedo bathing suit with spiky blond hair and an amazing tan. My sister and I found him highly entertaining and did our best to hang out with him. I didn't know he was an impersonator until the last night during the talent show, though. Prior to that, I just thought he was Rod Stewart.

There was a nightclub on the ship, and my dad gave them a credit card to keep open for the three-day stint. He told us to "go nuts," but I don't think he knew what we were capable of. At the time Jennifer was twenty, so she could legally drink since we were A) *on water* and B) *headed to Mexico.* I was still not old enough to drink, but my face was ahead of its time (a positive then, but now not so much), so nobody asked. We stayed up late every night with Fake Rod Stewart earning prestigious "Night Owl" badges and talking to people about all the athletes we'd rubbed elbows with in our short lives. Jennifer woke up every morning with a hangover; she was drinking specialty cocktails and frozen drinks. I woke up feeling fine; I was drinking bourbon and water. I knew better than to mix. My older sister was such a rookie.

When my father finally got his bar bill for the three days, he looked at us in shock. He went through each tab that was attached to it asking if that was one of our signatures. We confirmed all but one . . . one was Fake Rod Stewart's, *but we had told him that his drinks were on you, Dad.* I shut my eyes and waited for him to yell. My dad is a ton of fun, but when he gets mad it isn't pretty. I felt his hand on my shoulder and opened my eyes to see him smiling. "That's my girls," he said, then he signed the tab.

Toward the end of my summer visits with Dad I would start to miss my family and friends. I would usually get the pang when I still had a week or so left to go, making the last seven days almost unbearable. I'd spent enough time in the pool, at the beach, at nice restaurants and sporting events; now it was time to go home and tell everybody how much better my summer was than theirs.

We are all made up of two totally different people. Sometimes you live with them both, sometimes you don't. I don't know what it's like to live in an angry household, because my parents did the smart thing (in my opinion) when they knew it wasn't working: They walked away. Some people stay together for "the sake of the kids," but then the kids just get stuck thinking that people who are married are supposed to hate each other. My parents made sure I grew up in a house where people loved each other, even if for a few years it was just us girls. And even if one of them loved many different people.

No matter how we are raised or what values we are taught, we still have both of our parents' DNA. That's not a bad thing . . . it makes us who we are. I grew up in a small town. We canned our own green beans and fed apples to our horses on Christmas morning. It was a really nice life. It was a life you had if you raised a family, and you all lived close to each other, and you all remembered each other's birthday. It was completely different than the way it was at Dad's house. In his world people went to the beach and dressed up and had cocktail parties. I wanted to do that. I wanted to spend my own money on clothes that were too expensive and not have anybody yell at me about it.

Back home, watching parents drag kids to a spaghetti supper and knowing it was probably the highlight of their week freaked me out. They seemed happy, so why didn't I want it? One side of my family volunteered every day, at times putting their lives on the line to help others while I slumped around pissed off that I had to get up early on a Saturday. I felt like such an asshole. If someone wanted to live a perfectly normal Southern family life, who was I to judge? Something about the thought of it all made me cringe. I wasn't judging other people's happiness; I was judging myself for not understanding theirs. I couldn't put my finger on what it was that I didn't like about it. Whatever it was, I knew I had a different idea of fun and from what I understood, you couldn't take a baby to a bar.

## HYMEN GO SEEK

In Farmington there isn't a ton to do on the weekends. Well, there isn't a ton to do anytime. We had to make our own excitement. That usually meant driving out to a remote spot and drinking whatever we could get our hands on. When I turned sixteen I was actually able to buy beer myself instead of making someone's older sibling do it. I never got carded. That was something I was really proud of. It wasn't until much later that I figured out it was an insult.

I blame the fact that my face aged faster than me on the time I was visiting my dad in California and we fell asleep on the beach. I came back to Arkansas with a blistered face and my mom yelled about how she wasn't sure my face would ever recover.

"You might need surgery!" she yelled.

I was in a panic. It healed completely, but I've still always looked ten years older than I am. I'm positive it has *nothing* to do with smoking and drinking at an early age. No way.

My favorite place to hang out in high school was called Muddy Fork. It was a fork in the road, and it was muddy. There wasn't a lot of effort put into naming our hangouts, which is very similar to how my mother named our pets. We had a dog that liked to dig holes; his name was Digby. We had a cat that was afraid of everything; his name was Fraidy Cat. We had a kitten that we found that was tiny— "like a chigger," my mom said. So she named him Chigger. You get the idea. If you don't know what a chigger is, be grateful. They really itch.

Weekend destination spots had to be changed once the local cop caught on. It was always a sad moment. Lots of memories had been built in those places and we didn't want to have to start over. Also, we were lazy.

I remember distinctly the night that we had to leave Muddy Fork for good. My friend Jason was playing "Life Is a Highway" (not the Rascal Flatts version, the other one) on his brand-new fifteen-inch woofers. There was a period when I was in high school that the bigger your speakers, the bigger your popularity, so all the guys tried to outdo each other. He kept screaming "I'm gonna ride it all night long." I didn't know if he was talking about his truck or his drunk girlfriend, but he was loud. Blue lights flashed, we all got in our cars, and Muddy Fork was left in the dust. We always found a new place, though. After Muddy Fork we had the Power Lines, which, in retrospect, was incredibly unsafe.

The next destination that became popular was The Woods. It was a place in the woods. You'll catch on soon. The Woods was where we went after the Twin Bridges—the

spot in the middle of town with two bridges th
exactly the same—was no longer cool. We decide
bonfire there. You'd think coming from a family of volunteer firefighters I'd put up a little resistance to the idea, but
instead I just said "Hell yeah!" and helped throw wood and
trash into a huge pile. We had to stop going there one night
after a guy we called "Hippie" caught his face and ponytail
on fire when he tried to light the bonfire with a Bic lighter.

My favorite thing about high school was being on drill
team. I was pretty amazing at doing the Running Man so I
was a shoo-in the first year I auditioned. I took it pretty seriously.

The main reason to be on drill team instead of cheer-
leading was that the girls were a lot more fun than the cheerleaders, and by "fun" I mean "slutty." Also, you didn't have
to do a backflip, which I couldn't. Most of the cheerleaders
went to the Baptist church on Sundays and loved to talk
about their virginity. By the way, most of them got knocked
up right after high school. I guess holding off from sex for
four years made those girls go nuts the second they graduated. I was smart: I had sex in high school so that I knew
what I was doing once I got out in the real world.

Like any teenage girl, I had my share of heartbreaks.
Most of my high school years were spent in love with a guy
named Bucky. His real name was Daniel, but he preferred to
be called Bucky. His dad went by Butch and his brother
went by Buddy, so he isn't really to blame. He also didn't
even have buck teeth, so the whole nickname was a real
waste. In my defense, he was on the football team and he had
a mustache. You can't stop that kind of destiny. The Southern girl in me thought I needed to eventually settle down, be
stable and be in love, and Bucky was the one.

To this day, or at least to the day I finished this chapter, my mother still works at the funeral home. There aren't many in town, so pretty much everybody who has a family member who dies goes to Moore's Chapel. It's how I get to keep up with people from my past. She was *thrilled* to call me the day that Bucky came in for his aunt's funeral to tell me how things had turned out for him.

"From what it sounds like, he lives in a two-bedroom apartment with his wife and four children."

The Southern girl in me dodged a bullet.

Bucky was kind of a ladies' man, which was directly related to being able to grow a mustache at sixteen. He drove an El Camino because he thought it was mysterious. He believed that it was cool because nobody really knew if it was a car or a truck. He had a pair of the big woofer speakers like the other guys, but there wasn't a place to put them in an El Camino, so he had them installed behind the seat. Anytime I rode with him and he turned the music up I was thrown violently forward. But I just kept smiling.

He didn't seem to have a lot of interest in me at first, which made me really like him. We were "going together" on and off, but it took several rounds of dating for Bucky to finally refer to me as his girlfriend at school. Although my friends would try to tell me that he was not worth it, I just wrote it all off as commitment issues. I knew the type—my dad was one of them. Bucky just needed to play the field a little, but eventually he'd give in to our obvious passion and we would light the world on fire.

Even though we were technically together, I didn't feel like I really had Bucky's attention. I thought for sure there was something I wasn't giving him. I went through it over and over in my head and realized that the one thing I hadn't given him—my virginity—was standing in our way. If this relationship was going to go further, I was going to need to hand over my vagina.

Bucky chewed. It's common in the South. I've seen toddlers do it. His tobacco of choice was Copenhagen. Men who chew always keep a spit cup handy. They use the same one and empty it when it's full. It's disgusting. Bucky kept one in his bedroom on his windowsill. He said that way he could just dump it out when it was ready. It seemed to me it would have been much easier to just spit out the window.

Once I decided that he'd be my first, there was no going back. Almost all of the other girls in my class had already had sex, with the exception of the Baptists. I had waited long enough—I was fifteen and I wasn't getting any younger. Bucky was very open to the idea of being my first, so it didn't take much for him to come up with the place and time. His parents were going away for the weekend, and since he was seventeen and a senior in high school, they trusted him to be alone. We immediately planned our rendezvous.

I was nervous when I got to his place. I wasn't old enough to drive yet, so Lindsay dropped me off. This was one of the moments I was irritated that my mom put me in kindergarten when I was four. Apparently she couldn't wait to get me out of the house, but I hated being younger than all of my friends.

When we pulled up to Bucky's driveway, she and I sat silently in the car for a moment.

"You sure?" she asked.

"I'm sure," I told her.

"Make sure he wears something," she reminded me.

"If he forgets, I'll just take a long bath. Kristy says that works."

I got out of the car, tightened my scrunchie, smoothed out my floral spandex shorts, and headed for his front door. Lindsay backed slowly out of the driveway, and I could hear the *Thelma & Louise* soundtrack coming from her speakers.

"You're a part of me, I'm a part of you . . ." Glenn Frey crooned.

I turned to the front door and knocked. It was now or never.

Bucky answered the door wearing football pants and a do-rag. He smiled, spit into a plastic cup, and motioned for me to come in. I'd been in his house before, but this time everything seemed different. I knew his family didn't have a lot of money, but suddenly instead of "poor" they seemed "quaint." Instead of "dirty" the house just looked "unkempt." I was giving him excuses for the way that he lived. I still do that; I'm working on it. But at that point he was leading me to his bedroom. And I really needed to like him before we got there.

There was no time wasted on Bucky's side. I was there to fuck him, and he was in a time crunch. On the way to his room, he stopped only once, to show me his football helmet that his dad had mounted on the wall. On the front it said "Wheat." I didn't understand.

"Shouldn't you have gotten your name put on the front of the helmet? And if you wanted to use the name of a bread, why not everybody's favorite, 'Wonder'?"

He scoffed at my ignorance. "Wheat is short for Buckwheat, which was derived from Bucky, which is my name."

"Actually your name is Daniel."

"My name is Bucky."

"Bucky is a nickname. You nicknamed your nickname?"

"Whatever, Miss Straight-A's. Let's go get down."

We continued on to the bedroom and Bucky pushed the door open, then stepped aside so that I could enter. The smell of chewing tobacco wafted past me. Bucky led me by the hand to his bed. I was in a daze. He gently pushed me down, then awkwardly fell on top of me. He was pretty heavy and I couldn't breathe.

"So . . . heavy . . . just can you . . . ouch," I muttered. My air was being cut off.

"Sorry, baby." Then he moved more to the side. "Hold on, I have a surprise for you."

Bucky stood up and went to his dresser. He got out a condom and winked at me. He then rummaged through a few cassette tapes, found the one he wanted, and popped it into his ghetto blaster. He pushed "play" and the lyrics to Too $hort's "Don't Fight the Feelin'" filled the room:

*Say ho*
*yeah you*
*Can I ask you a question*
*You like to fuck?*
*Oh, you don't want me to talk to you like that*
*Will you like to make love?*

"Our song," Bucky whispered into my ear. I racked my brain trying to remember why this was our song. It didn't seem that romantic. I was also pretty sure we didn't have a song.

*I saw you walking down the street, and I had to stop*
*Turn up the radio and drop the top*
*I see you look so good, and you're so fine*
*Young tender, would you be mine. . . .*

I shook my head. "I don't think this is our song."

"Of course it is. It's always the song that is *our* song when I have a girlfriend."

"So it's *your* song and when you have a girlfriend it's *their* song, too?"

"Not *their* song, it's our song."

"But then it isn't our song if it's your song with all of your ex-girlfriends." I started to tear up. This wasn't going as planned.

"No, baby, this is for you. I've never played it for a virgin before," he said proudly.

Suddenly he was on top of me. He pulled down his pants, then mine, and before I knew what was happening I had lost my virginity. I looked up and noticed that he had knocked his spit cup over. Brown saliva trickled down his window as the Too $hort song continued:

*Your name is yuck mouth, you don't brush*
*Gotta cover your mouth like this*
*They call you yuck mouth*
*You refuse to brush, no sweetheart you can keep that*
    *kiss.*

I wriggled to get free from Bucky's grasp. This was really embarrassing. I just wanted to get out of the way of the fallen saliva moving directly toward my head. Unfortunately I didn't make it in time. Bucky jumped up and got me a towel, one of the only caring things he'd done that day, and probably during our entire relationship. Right after he wiped his armpits with it, he handed me the towel to clean the spit off my face.

If you've never had sex for the first time with someone

playing trashy rap with a mouth full of chew, keep it that way. I passed it off as fine because I had nothing to compare it to. Now the whole thing reminds me of a crime scene. I still have nightmares.

From that night on, Bucky and I became a real couple. Much like Ricky Walden, he didn't waste time telling people at school what had occurred between us the night before. I had every right to be upset with him, but I wasn't. He pacified the whole thing by presenting me with his class ring. It was about ten sizes too big for me. I wrapped tons of yarn around the base of it so that it would fit my finger. I decided that him giving me his ring meant that me giving him my hymen was okay. We were officially together. The only thing that scared me was that he was a senior and I was a junior. I couldn't imagine what school would be like next year without him.

When I turned sixteen and needed my first job, Bucky put in a word for me where he was working, which was at Hardee's. It felt really romantic to be working side by side with my boyfriend. We were in the trenches together. We already had Friday night football and now we had fast food.

I started as a cashier. I took people's orders and filled their bags with cheeseburgers and thanked them for choosing Hardee's. It didn't take long for me to get restless; I really wanted to work the drive-thru. Bucky scoffed at me.

"Everybody wants to work drive-thru. That's where the respect is."

"Okay, well, can you train me? I think I can pick it up pretty fast. I hate working the counter. It's too much interacting with people." Later in life, when I had to wait tables for a good fifteen years, this would really wear on me.

"You're joking, right?" Bucky asked. "You think you

can just waltz in here and work drive-thru? You ain't even done fry detail yet. Just wait your turn."

I couldn't understand what the big deal was. I wanted to wear that headset so bad. I couldn't stand having to talk to people face-to-face anymore. Plus, at the drive-thru window you could slip free burgers and drinks to your friends. It was a position of power.

Bucky wasn't a ton of help in moving me up at work. He told the manager that I should learn to make biscuits like everyone else. For weeks I had to come in to work at 5 A.M. on Saturdays and Sundays to fill aluminum trays with biscuit mix. It was much worse than the breakfasts at the fire department. At least at those all I had to do was serve. Now suddenly I was a cook, too? *This is bullshit.*

At school we had something called "Colors Day." It was like homecoming, but for basketball. I was voted onto the "Colors Day Court" as a Junior Maid. This was a really big fucking deal in my mind. It meant people liked me. It meant that even though I wasn't one of the Baptists, I was accepted. I had to buy a nice dress, get my hair done, and have someone to dance with during the "royalty number" at the big dance that took place after school. Of course, I asked Bucky.

Between the game, having to sit on a makeshift throne for three hours, and the dance, I felt wiped out from my big evening. I went home immediately after the dance, opting to skip the after party at Rhonda Lewis's house. Bucky said he was still going to go; my exhaustion certainly didn't need to ruin his good time.

The next morning Bucky came wandering in to Hardee's with a giant hickey on his neck.

"What the fuck is that?" I yelled the second that I saw him.

"What?"

"*That.*" I pointed to the purple bruise. "That *hickey*. What did you do!" I started to cry.

"Oh, that. That's not a hickey. Clint Pearson and I were messing around, and he pinched me."

"Clint Pearson doesn't have a thumb," I yelled. "You can't effectively pinch somebody if you don't have a thumb!"

I dragged Bucky back into dry storage and demanded the truth. He confessed that he had made out with Rhonda Lewis. I was appalled. Rhonda Lewis was the most unattractive, manliest-looking girl you could ever imagine. Back then she was the queen of the basketball courts and I'm sure by now she's the queen of some other woman's vagina.

I became enraged. I started throwing thirty-two-ounce plastic Teenage Mutant Ninja Turtles cups at him and calling him every name in the book, including Daniel, because I knew that would really get under his skin.

Having your boyfriend cheat on you at sixteen is devastating, especially when he is your first and you're still trying to figure out how to get on the pill without telling your mom. You feel like all of the trust and air has been taken out of you. There was no way I was going to be the dumb girl that worked it out with my crappy boyfriend. I was simply going to move on and have sex with another guy as soon as possible to put this whole thing behind me.

Bucky was not happy that I broke up with him over the "incident" with Rhonda Lewis. Suddenly he was madly in love with me and couldn't bear to face the idea of losing me. He stalked, called, and wrote terrible poetry that he left on my car. I saved all of them. I was sure I'd need them one day in court, or in a book about how dumb I was. Here's to the latter:

I love you very much
For when we go out we won't go dutch . . .
Don't eat my shit
So I can lick your tit . . .
I have wrecked our lives
As if with knives . . .
So I depart
With a Fart . . .

*Is that an apology?* I was sure that he was losing his mind. He called me crying, begging for us to get back together. He said I should be his wife and we were meant to be. I don't know what turned him this way; I assume it was guilt. I think it's common for people to take things for granted until they're gone, which was something I had learned from the band Cinderella and their song "Don't Know What You Got (Till It's Gone)." Bucky was also just about to graduate from high school and no colleges were interested in his 2.7 GPA or his barely impressive football skills. He was coming unraveled.

I was becoming slightly unraveled too, but I didn't know it. I started paying attention to the Baptists at school. Those girls seemed so happy. They didn't ever look hungover, and I was pretty sure none of them had ever had a urinary tract infection, which I was certain I had gotten because Bucky had been unfaithful. One Sunday I suggested to Lindsay that we attend the First Baptist Church.

Sitting in that church was an odd experience. Suddenly all the Baptists were saying hello to me, much more friendly than usual. They were welcoming me and Lindsay and letting us know that if we needed anything, to call them. I thanked them but assured them I wouldn't need to call. I knew where the church was and as long as I showed up on Sundays, shit would start turning around for me.

The second time I went, I cried throughout the whole sermon. It felt like the right thing to do. At the end the preacher asked if anybody needed to be saved. I started having flashbacks to my night with Penny. I crossed my fingers and prayed that people didn't start writhing on the floor. Then I felt myself stand up. I raised my hand and walked toward the front of the church. I needed to be saved. *I have sinned*. I wasn't supposed to have sex, let alone a bladder infection. Maybe the preacher could wash all of that away. I turned to look for Lindsay and she was following me. I smiled—we were in this together.

Getting dunked backward into a tub of lukewarm water was not something I was expecting to do that day. I was definitely not dressed for it. There were plenty of people who I knew that were in attendance, and now I was committing to a religion I barely knew anything about right in front of them. Regardless, Lindsay and I were both officially cleared of our sins and could start our lives over.

I got home, dripping wet, and told Mom that I was an official member of the Baptist Church. I hoped she wasn't going to be mad. She was Methodist and I didn't want her to feel I was going against her, even though I had no idea if I had.

"Do you know what it means to be Baptist?" she asked.

"Sort of."

She looked like she had something to say, but she bit her tongue. "You're free to believe in anything you want to believe in. But I suggest you put on a new T-shirt before you catch a cold."

I went to church for a couple more weeks. I knew that

Farmington was a "dry" town but you could buy alcohol when you got five miles down the road into Fayetteville. I also knew that in both towns no liquor was sold on Sunday. I used to solve that by driving to Missouri on Sundays to buy beer. It would have been easier to just stock up on Saturday nights, but that was my way of not accepting the rules. It was not until I went to church and started hanging out with the Baptists that I realized *they* were responsible for the weird liquor rules. They had a lot of rules that I was not expecting, but I was trying to roll with it.

One day the pastor told me that I was going to have to quit drill team. I thought he was joking.

Apparently Baptists in Farmington didn't believe in dancing. I explained to him that it was my senior year and that I'd probably make captain, which is as prestigious as you can get. Surely he didn't expect me to hang up my pom-pons for a church, especially this late in the game. He explained that in his religion, which was now my religion, they don't believe in dancing for amusement; it had to be for a purpose.

"It is for a purpose. It's for halftime," I fired back.

He wouldn't budge. "It just isn't something that we can condone."

"But all of the cheerleaders are Baptists. How'd they get around this?"

"They don't dance. They cheer," he said confidently.

"But they do the splits and climb on top of each other to make a pyramid. Is that for a purpose?"

He sighed and told me to make my decision. I was furious. I thought about all of our school dances. Those girls were always there, and always dancing. When nobody was watching, they did what they wanted. The pastor didn't show up for dances, but he sure showed up for the football games. I felt like I was surrounded by a bunch of hypocrites.

There was no way I was giving up the one thing I loved doing to keep a bunch of people from sneering at me. I was pretty sure that God didn't care if I did the Running Man. I figured He just wanted me to be a good person.

I decided that my relationship with God was solid enough that I could dance and believe in him at the same time. I'd seen *Footloose* and I didn't have a train yard to run out to and do my routine in in secret, so I just stopped going to church. I didn't really quit that church just to remain on drill team, even if that is a better story. I quit because I felt like people weren't honest about what they did when they weren't in church. I don't see the point of only believing in something on Sundays.

My senior year I made captain. My team gave me a whistle with my name engraved on it, which I wore proudly. I was still getting hounded by Bucky, but at least he'd graduated so he wasn't at school every day. He occasionally left notes on my car, but it was not as frequent since it now required a special trip for him.

I started dating a guy named Tony. He and I were good friends but he was also close with Bucky. We decided to be together, even though we knew it was going to affect their friendship. Tony told me that our song was "(Everything I Do) I Do It for You" by Bryan Adams. It was used in the movie *Robin Hood* and it was all about how a guy's love for this woman was worth fighting for, just like Tony thought ours was. I didn't think it was a perfect song choice but in the romance department it certainly beat anything by Too $hort.

"Is that our song or is that your song with all of your girlfriends?" I challenged.

"What? It's *our* song. What kind of person would have the same song for every girlfriend?"

I kissed him.

Bucky heard about me and Tony, but neither of us would admit to him that it was true. Because of that, Bucky spent his free time trying to prove it. When our class took a trip to the state fair, he tailed the bus hoping to catch Tony and me hanging out together. He was behind us the whole time, thinking nobody would notice him. He still drove an El Camino—everybody noticed. He even went into the fair and attempted to talk to me. Every time I looked behind me, he was approaching. We just kept turning corners to lose him. I'd run into a bathroom while Tony got in line for a funnel cake. I was so embarrassed, and all I really wanted was to ride the Tilt-A-Whirl.

Finally Bucky's letters to me became so rambling and off track that I told Tony I thought he might be clinically insane or on drugs. Tony said that he didn't think Bucky was on drugs.

"Did he ever do any around you?"

"No way," I explained. "I won't tolerate any drugs."

"But I smoke pot," he said.

"Oh, pot is fine. I smoke that sometimes when I'm in the mood. I just won't do drug-drugs."

"Like what? Cocaine?"

"Cocaine is the worst! Have you ever read any of the Sweet Valley High novels? In one of them this girl Regina decided to try cocaine for the first time and her heart stopped. I mean, she died the first time she tried it! I told Bucky about that, so I don't think he'd ever do cocaine. Did you read that one?"

"Can't say that I have read any of those. Sounds pretty intense."

"Oh, you have no idea. You can borrow some if you want. I have them all."

"I'm good. I don't really like books."

Eventually I broke up with Tony. I knew I was going to college the next year and I didn't want to be tied down. I had big dreams and I couldn't let a man stand in my way. I also knew Tony was not going to college, since you couldn't major in pot. I decided to spare him what I went through when I was a sophomore and Brent Jackson went away to college. We had tried to stay boyfriend and girlfriend but eventually we grew apart. I was not interested in a boyfriend who couldn't be in town to take me to PG-13 movies and Taco Bell.

When graduation day finally came around, my dad was a no-show. He had always said that he'd be there, but work was too busy and he couldn't make it. I was disappointed, but I sort of got it. What was he going to do in Farmington? He wore a suit and tie and was probably afraid of cowboy hats. And it was a long trip for something not that rare; most people in the world accomplish graduating at some point. It actually taught me a good lesson: If you have kids, you may unknowingly disappoint them. It seemed like it was smarter to not overcommit yourself, then nobody could say you'd let them down. If you do what you want to do, you're the only person who can feel slighted.

Bucky still didn't give up when I started college. He heard, most likely through a phone tap, that Tony and I had broken it off. He thought now that I was out of high school maybe we could start dating again. I don't think he realized that starting college meant I was moving forward rather than backward. He heard I was majoring in theater, so he called me up and told me that he was going to audition for a local production of *Romeo and Juliet*.

"They are holding auditions soon. I think I'd be a good Romeo since I have a lot of love in me. Plus I'm good at football."

"But Romeo doesn't play football . . ."

"He does now."

I don't have to explain to you what a rather large man with a mustache would look like running around in tights trying to speak in iambic pentameter. But since the only thing Bucky ever followed through on was not leaving me alone, the audition never happened.

After many phone calls I gave in and agreed to meet him for lunch. I was no longer working at Hardee's. I had moved on to a respectable job at a real restaurant named Bert's Grill & Bakery. It was like a chain restaurant, but *not* a chain. The owner was a recovering alcoholic, so the place didn't serve alcohol. I always thought that was really selfish of him; it wasn't his customers' fault that he couldn't control himself around tequila. I decided Bert's would be a good place to meet Bucky for lunch. Since I hadn't seen him in about a year, a public place where I knew people seemed like the right call.

When he walked in my stomach sank. He had a big fat gut and his mustache looked like it was growing toward it. I couldn't remember why I had agreed to this meeting. He greeted me with a big smile and I attempted one in return. I then told him we should sit down before it got busy, which was code for "Let's get in and out of here before anybody else spots us."

We sat down at the table and one of my co-workers, Logan, came to take our order. He and I were good friends so I asked him to take care of us in case shit started to go south.

I immediately started to wonder if Bucky had ever been to a sit-down restaurant before. Questions like "What would you like on your baked potato?" and "What kind of dressing do you want on your salad?" threw him for a loop. He looked at me with panic in his eyes. He just kept answering, "Ranch."

"You want ranch dressing on your baked potato?" Logan asked with a smirk.

"Yes, unless you think Thousand Island is better."

I took over the ordering. "Just give him a baked potato with everything on it. And see if they can rush the food."

I could tell Logan was getting a real kick out of the whole situation. In fact, all of the waiters snickered in the back, asking me who my date was. I should have taken him to a place that was dark and quiet and nobody knew who I was. When Bucky got up to use the restroom, I told Logan that he'd been in an accident and that he had suffered brain damage.

"I'm so sorry, Sarah. I didn't realize. But it explains a lot."

"It's fine. Just please tell the others not to laugh at him. It's rude," I warned.

I suffered through the meal, finding comfort in knowing that this would be the last time I saw him. He suffered through his baked potato, uncertain why tiny green things were chopped up on top of it. I attempted to explain what a chive was but gave up when he said he had once gotten the chives from taking medication.

I guess he didn't realize how poorly the whole thing went because he still called a few times after. Eventually he gave up, the clincher being when I changed my phone number. He left word through our mutual friends that I was missing out. He was going to be extremely successful with his new venture, which was the opening of a venetian blind cleaning business.

# FRIENDS WITHOUT BENEFITS

It was only a fifteen-minute drive to the University of Arkansas in Fayetteville from my parents' house in Farmington, but once I discovered Café Santa Fe's Long Island Iced Teas served by the carafe, that drive became way too long. I had one of my sister's expired driver's licenses but, as usual, I never had to use it since nobody ever asked me for my ID. A taxi was definitely not something that you could just grab, especially to Farmington. In fact, the only consistently reliable source of public transportation in Fayetteville was the Fayetteville Trolley, and that only took you up and down the town square. Fun when you're drunk, but not functional for getting a lift home. I had another option of a place to crash, since I was having sex with one of the waiters who worked at Café Santa Fe. When you're eighteen and you don't have to pay for your own drinks, thirty-something waiters named Gary can be irresistible. Unfortunately that ended abruptly one night when we were having sex and he pulled a gun out from underneath his pillow and laid it on my chest.

"Oh my God, are you going to kill me?"

"No, I just think guns are sexy. Don't you?"

"No."

"Well, that's too bad."

"So now are you going to kill me?"

We didn't go out for long.

If I was going to continue to have college-style fun while still maintaining my status as a daughter who had her shit together, I was going to need to get my own place. Plus I was getting too old to be calling my mother and asking her if it was cool to crash on a friend's couch.

One of the best things about college was the people I met. I had two different worlds. In my classes, I had people around me who had similar dreams of acting and doing stand-up and going to Hollywood. Working at Bert's, I had a bunch of sorority girls and fraternity guys around me who had similar dreams of finishing our shifts and getting drunk. Like Patrick, who went to the walk-in cooler every Sunday morning and sniffed all of the nitrous oxide out of the cans of whipped cream.

When I hung out with my work friends I went to awful parties and carried around red plastic cups. When I hung out with my theater friends I went to awful parties and carried around badly rolled joints. After play rehearsals we would go to the bar down the street from the theater, named Fuzzy's, where they had giant frozen beer mugs and served pitchers for three dollars. There was one guy named Marty in our group who only had money once a month, when he got paid from a job. Nobody understood what he did but we knew it involved a tractor. We'd all buy his drinks for three weeks, then on payday he'd take us to Fuzzy's and spend his entire paycheck. Then the next day he'd be penniless again and the cycle would start all over. After work at Bert's, we'd go to a place called My Pleasure, a dark and loungey bar that served drinks with various fruit garnishes and you had to sign a guest book to get in.

These were the kinds of people I was dealing with, and I liked it. I never brought a theater friend to a work party, and vice versa. I rarely mixed the two groups together; the thought of it gave me a rash. I discovered that in college, with these two groups of friends, I could be who I wanted to be at any given time. It was similar to having the two different parents. On some nights I was the girl who was serious about theater and life goals and loved to read plays, and on other nights I was the girl who was serious about getting laid and mastering a keg stand. Both of those girls were me but I didn't feel confident that one side would be accepted by the other. I figured out my own way to balance it all—work, friends, fun, and school. Or so I thought. Later in life I'd find that balancing those things while trying to maintain a real relationship would also be a challenge.

Just when I was about to lose my mind living at home, one of the girls I worked with at Bert's told me that she was about to have an empty spot in her four-bedroom house. Caryn was a sorority girl, and so were her roommates. Those girls were fun to drink with on a Saturday night, but I didn't know if I'd want to wake up to them every day—kind of like how I felt about most guys I'd met. What I did know was that these girls lived within walking distance of Dickson Street, where all the bars were.

As far as the house went, everything was perfect. My share of the rent was $150, which seemed like a lot then but now seems ridiculous. The house had the four bedrooms, a big kitchen, two bathrooms, washer and dryer—everything. I was envisioning my first big summer party and how good I'd be at keg stands by October.

Caryn was one of the nicest people I'd ever met. She was also one of those people who wore Christmas sweaters with pine trees and bells on them—even in July. She also loved to wear these big cow slippers that went "moo" with every step she took. We shared the same side of the house, along with the same bathroom, yet she would always seem surprised when I'd get up early on days that I didn't have class.

One morning I was particularly hungover and she found me standing outside the bathroom with a look of death on my face.

"What are you doing up?" she asked me. She was all smiles, fresh from the shower.

"Really?" I asked. "Fucking really?" I had woken up thinking that there was a herd of cows inside my bedroom.

I picked up one of her slippers that was lying by the bathroom door and stuck it in the toilet. Without saying a word, I went back to sleep. From then on Caryn wore normal, quiet slippers—and avoided me in the mornings.

Leanne and Shannon were my other new roommates. Shannon was this blond, sweet girl who fooled you into thinking she was low-key but could drink more than me on a bad summer cruise. We sat up night after night drinking whatever was left in the house. Leanne was the loud one.

She was on the rifle team in high school and loved to get drunk and perform her routine to the *Grease* soundtrack with a broomstick. She'd spin and twirl it until every person and every thing in our house had to run for cover. During our time at that house, we went through a lot of lamps.

Leanne seemed like a lesbian to me and to most other people, but she insisted that she liked men. She always said that she didn't want a boyfriend because her heart was once broken and that she was just "not interested." She is now out of the closet, very happy, and can still twirl the hell out of a broom.

I became best friends with one of the guys I worked with at Bert's. His name was Andy. He and I did everything together, from movies to drinks to taking quizzes in *Cosmo*. He was the perfect gay best friend, only straight. I couldn't remember having a friend like Andy since I had graduated from high school. I didn't even realize at the time that I had already put most people from high school behind me. I had outgrown them in less than a year. You'd think I would have felt more of a loss for the people I'd been going to school with for the past seven or so years of my life, but I didn't. I just moved on. I've never been one to hang on to the past. I don't have coffee with exes, and I certainly don't check in from time to time to "see how things are going." Plus this was the new me, the college me. It was the fall of 1992 and I had college friends. High school was so six months ago.

The only loss I really felt was my friendship with Lindsay. Since we'd graduated, she and I had completely drifted apart. She got pregnant and married right after high school; I don't remember in which order. We tried to hang out a few times, but her husband would always get mad before she even left the house. He had this idea that I was a bad influence on her, which was stupid. We didn't urge each other on like some bad after-school special; we were just girls who grew up in a small town. I actually tried really hard to bond with her husband when they got together our senior year. I even had sex with his brother a couple of times, and that guy had some issues and was really into rodeos. I was being a really good friend to put myself in that kind of position. He wasn't impressed.

I noticed Lindsay was starting to take on her husband's attitude toward me. She would ask in a really condescending tone what I was doing out so late the night before. She was judging me because I had chosen a different life than she did. One day she randomly called and asked me when I was going to grow up.

"I just started college, so probably not for a few more years," I replied, annoyed.

"Well, don't you think it's time you started acting like an adult?"

"I'm eighteen. I'm not supposed to yet."

"Eighteen is when you become an adult," she lectured.

"No, eighteen is when some people are forced to become an adult because their boyfriend doesn't believe in birth control."

We didn't talk much after that. I didn't need or want to be judged by people who were convinced that the way they lived their lives was the only way. To this day I don't have time for people like that. It stung to lose her, but we were going in different directions.

Andy filled the void I felt that Lindsay had left and suddenly I had the new Thelma to my Louise, although he wouldn't let me call him that. We were inseparable. The only time I can remember us even fighting was over the name of those Little Debbie cakes that are round and white with black stripes. Zebra Cakes, by the way. And they're delicious.

Since Andy also worked at Bert's, he knew Caryn. I started to notice a spark between them, so I got really excited at the idea of setting them up.

I don't know if you've ever been in love with someone, not realized it, and then set them up with your roommate. I don't recommend it. The second Andy and Caryn started to date, I was in hell. The two of them together were nauseating. I asked everyone else I knew why they were so annoying, but nobody seemed to see it. I was the only one bothered by their union. *Oh, shit . . .*

As girly as Caryn was, she loved to fart. I've never understood that. I won't even talk about going number two if a guy is around, let alone do it. I'd prefer to suffer silently and cause permanent damage to my colon. Caryn was the complete opposite. She farted all the time around Andy, and I could tell he hated it. It really seemed to turn him off, so I encouraged her to keep doing it.

"Guys love when you are just yourself!" I told her. "Don't hold back anything—he wants to feel like you're one of the guys. Plus I've read that it's bad for you to hold it in!"

One day Andy told me he was starting to feel like Caryn was just one of the guys rather than his girlfriend. He told me she farted in front of him. I told him she was probably manic-depressive. I was doing all I could.

I attempted to keep my mind off being in love with my best friend by sleeping with other guys. The first guy I used as a distraction was named Max. He was flawless. Gorgeous. Complete with a blond ponytail (when that was in). He was a frat boy *and* he waited tables at Fuzzy's, so flirting with him often landed me a free pitcher or two of beer. I guess I had a thing for waiters when I was in college, but at least this one never pulled a gun on me.

I noticed that broke Marty would always offer to pay when Max was working, even when it wasn't his pay week. Obviously he'd caught on to the freebies I was getting and figured that if he offered but there was no bill to pay, he'd still get credit for offering. I couldn't get mad at him. It was actually kind of ingenious.

Max was the unattainable hot waiter to pretty much everyone who went in to Fuzzy's. It never even occurred to me that he would look my way, especially then—I had a particularly awful haircut. I have thick, curly hair so cutting it off above my ears was a terrible mistake. My friend dubbed it "The Ma'am," because it looked just like Ma'am's haircut from the TV show *Webster*. Google it—not pretty. At some point Max asked me out and I accepted, but I was still confused. All I wanted to do was find and tell Andy. Now I would have a hot guy and Andy would have Caryn and her flatulence problem, along with the latest fabrication I'd told him about her: a history of gout.

Max and I went on our date. He turned out to be pretty dumb. He was really, really sweet, but then again most dumb people are. He didn't get my sense of humor at all, which was a real bummer considering at the time it was my best asset. During my date with Max I made several cracks that fell flat and he stared at me like I had just given him a math quiz. It was so frustrating. That was the first time I'd experienced how disappointing it can be when the only good quality a hot guy has is that he's hot. That had always seemed like it would be a great thing. I even started to resent his ponytail, which thus far had been one of my favorite features. I began to tune him out and stare at it. I wondered why he had such a luxurious mane when my hair was too short and was growing up toward the sun like a mushroom. I finally decided that since this was going nowhere we should just get back to his apartment and have sex. That seemed like the least I could do for the other girls and gay men who hung out with me at Fuzzy's and wanted to know all about his penis. It was pretty great, but I still didn't go out with him again. I did hold a lot of pride knowing that I was the only theater girl who could land this guy, though. The next morning I'd woken up in a frat house positive that no other girl from my "Acting Shakespeare" class ever had.

Shortly after that, I dated a guy named Tom, who was on the swim team. He was a diver. He had an ass like a grapefruit. *Screw it,* I thought. *Maybe this haircut is really working for me.* I couldn't wait to have sex with Tom so that I could tell Andy about it. That's never a great sign. He and Caryn were still dating, although I was pretty sure that the new information I had just given him about her genital warts was starting to get to him. He really wanted to talk to her about it, but I assured him that she had them frozen off so he wasn't susceptible to them.

"It's best not to bring it up. It'll just embarrass her."

The first time I slept with Tom he told me he didn't have a condom but that he did have shampoo.

"Most of the ingredients in shampoo are the same that are in spermicide," he explained.

I just wanted to have sex with him. Andy and I had plans the next day and I needed the story. So I accepted his explanation and we went at it. I kept thinking about my friend Kristy from high school and how she really did believe that baths helped to prevent pregnancies. Somewhere, somehow, the school system was failing us. Tom wasn't a dumb guy, though. He was just using the same strategy to get me to have sex with him as I was using to get Andy and Caryn to stop having sex: lying. For that reason, I couldn't blame him. I'm just grateful that the only thing I got out of that night was a well-conditioned vagina.

Tom was cute and fun, passionate and smart, and he thought I was funny. It felt like maybe he was the kind of guy I needed. Perhaps he could get me over Andy. I appreciated that he had focus, even though I felt that diving was an unreliable choice for a college major.

The next day at lunch Andy asked me how things were going with the diver.

"Amazing," I exaggerated. "We had sex last night. He's really got some moves. I guess all that underwater breathing pays off."

"What does that mean?"

I wasn't expecting that. "Um, you figure it out!"

"Well, I'm glad it's going well. But do you think that diving is really a great life plan?"

"I don't know. Is *not* diving a great life plan? Because that's what you're doing!"

"What?"

"Exactly."

At one point there was some sort of uproar regarding the swim team. They weren't getting funded, or they were losing their funds, or maybe they just weren't fun. I never really knew what the problem was, I just wore a button that said SAVE OUR SWIM TEAM (SOS for short) and got really mad when people didn't know why I wore it. Those people would then ask me to explain what was going on and since I couldn't I'd just say, "Try paying attention to what's happening at your own school!" I didn't even know we had a swim team until I met Tom, so I was definitely the asshole. It didn't really matter; if I wanted to keep my cute new boyfriend to combat my feelings for my roommate's boyfriend, whom I had set her up with and who was also my best friend, I needed the swim team at the University of Arkansas to get whatever the fuck it was they needed.

I wore my SOS button like my life depended on it. I even attended a couple of rallies where I yelled out things like "You got that right," even though I didn't know what "that" was. It was all becoming a little daunting. I wasn't even that into this guy and now I was running around like Sally Field in *Norma Rae* but unlike her I didn't give a shit about whatever my cause was. In only a matter of weeks, I started to get annoyed with Tom. Watching him in his Speedos at practice went from adorable to stupid to gross. I couldn't take this guy seriously anymore. I was nearing the end of my years as an official teen and I needed to find a provider, not someone who could simply nail a pike position. I ended things with him and went back to focusing on my classes and school. This relationship crap was not working out.

Caryn and Andy continued to date. I continued to get drunk. I found myself crying when they were together at our house parties, claiming that it was because we had run out of onion dip. I mean I *was* always really disappointed when that happened—it is my favorite party dip—but the tears were not from that. I could tell that Andy wasn't really happy in the relationship, but some part of him thought he had to continue to date her. I don't remember if he ever seemed very happy, though. He was pretty lost. He didn't really know what he wanted to do with his life and it bothered him. Maybe he didn't really *need* to know at the time, but I felt like he never would.

The night he told me he was going to break up with Caryn I was confused. I expected to be really happy, but I wasn't. I looked at my friend, who I loved, and thought about how now we could have our chance. Then I pictured my other friend, who I also loved, and thought about how sad she was going to feel. I knew she really cared about Andy, and I certainly couldn't blame her. I ruled out telling him we should see what it felt like to dry-hump and tried to focus on giving him good advice. I needed to put my own feelings aside and be a good friend to both of them. I suggested he just be honest. We talked for a long time, and he seemed satisfied that he knew the right way to let her down gently. He got up to go, but I grabbed his hand and stopped him. *Shit.* I was doing so well at being neutral. Now his hand was in mine and he was waiting to hear what I had to say that was so important that it made me stop him on his way out the door.

"What is it?" he asked.

"I just . . . go easy on her. You're going to be hard for her to lose," I told him.

"Don't make me feel worse."

I sat there silent, struggling to fight back what I really wanted to say to him—how I knew he'd be hard to be without because I went through it every day. How he and I would be a great couple. How I was in love with him and if we just waited, Caryn would understand. How we should seriously see what it felt like to dry-hump.

"Do you think I'm making a mistake, Sarah?"

"Not at all. It's just . . . I found a bottle of toe fungus cream in her bathroom cabinet. I think she's probably really sensitive right now. That can be embarrassing to have, especially in the summer."

Andy made a grossed-out face and left. I felt bad for a second, but toe fungus wasn't as bad as some of the other things I could have made up. At least I didn't say what I wanted to say and now things between us would still be normal. I knew that Caryn was going to be okay eventually. He and I belonged together, and if what I heard about soul mates was true, then he couldn't be hers because he was mine, and now that he would be free to be mine, she'd be free to meet hers. It's called a favor.

As expected, Caryn was sad for a while after they broke up. But she also was one of those girls who fell for a guy right away, so I knew once she went on a date with someone else she'd be really into him. I wasn't sure that was so great for the next guy, but it was great for everybody else and I hadn't met this imaginary guy yet so his happiness wasn't my problem.

A few months later, Andy and I were out in my sad white Mustang. It wasn't one of the cool Mustangs, it was the other kind—used, with cracked red vinyl seats. I don't even know how the conversation started; it just did. We'd had a fun night out for Andy's roommate Joby's birthday. We were all sitting in the car listening to Mötley Crüe and singing along to "Home Sweet Home," which is probably where we should have gone. Joby had gotten so drunk that when I said anything to him he couldn't respond so he'd just lick my face. It was like having a drunk dog in the backseat.

Andy and I dropped Joby off at their place and carried him to bed. I tried to explain to Andy that he needed to sleep on his side so that if he vomited in his sleep he wouldn't choke to death. Andy explained that if Joby vomited, there was a good chance he'd wake up and go do it in the bathroom, or at least in the trash can we'd planted next to his bed. I reminded him that my mom worked at a funeral home and that he should listen to me.

"Why? Has she told you that someone died because he choked on his vomit?" he asked, slightly panicked.

I thought for a few moments. "No."

"Then what are you talking about?"

"I don't know. But she does work at a funeral home. Let's go get some Taco Bell."

We picked up Taco Bell then went to the park to sit and eat it in the car. No wonder my car always smelled disgusting. The park was the college equivalent of what The Woods or the Power Lines were for me in high school—where we all ended up after a night out.

We started talking and both admitted we had feelings for the other. I was elated. That wore off quickly when he brought up that he was worried about telling our other friends. I was worried, too, but he could have at least let me enjoy the combination of our revelation and a Beef Burrito Supreme (hold the tomato) for a minute.

"Caryn might be hurt," I confirmed, "but she does already have a new boyfriend that she's really into."

"Really?" he asked, surprised.

"Why, are you jealous or something? If you still like her I don't want to even have this conv—"

"I don't still like her, Sarah. I like you. I'm just surprised; I hadn't heard."

"Okay. Well, I'm about eighty-seven percent sure he's gay, but I figure I should stay out of it. She's already going to be pissed at me."

The guy I was referring to is now out of the closet and very happy. Maybe I should have majored in outing people.

Andy and I went back to my house that night, and nobody was there. We lay on my bed, like we'd done a hundred times before, but this time we were looking at each other differently. In the past it had always been platonic, and now we were thinking about making it unplatonic. (Yes, I just made that a word.) He leaned in to kiss me, and we both started laughing. He tried again, and we laughed. I tried to lead the kiss—we giggled uncontrollably. This was a nightmare. At least it was affecting us both this way, or the other person would have been really offended.

"What is our problem?" I asked.

"I don't know. I guess it's just weird. It's weird to think we are going to kiss." He sighed.

"Kiss? I was sort of hoping we were going to have sex," I told him.

He just looked at me.

I rolled my eyes. "God, I'm kidding," I said, even though I wasn't. "We can't do it right away; it's too soon," even though I had totally thought that was the plan.

Finally we leaned in to each other and successfully kissed. We busted out laughing afterward, but at least we managed to get our tongues in each other's mouths.

"Well, that's done. Maybe we should go ahead and get the fucking over with, too," I said.

He just looked at me.

"God, I was kidding! It's way too soon for that!" I laughed even though up to that point that was the only thing on my mind.

We got under the covers and fell asleep together. It actually felt kind of good to just curl up with him and not have him tugging on my underwear. My heart was beating so fast

I thought it was going to come out of my chest. Suddenly I had the feeling that my life was going to work out. *I already have my guy.*

The next couple of weeks were filled with telling our friends we were a couple and trying to adjust to what it meant for us to date. Caryn actually took it pretty well, although she wanted to know how long I had feelings for him. It took a lot for me to do it, but I told her the truth. I was just glad that we could still be friends, so it seemed like I owed her that. I left out the part about how I once told him that she had Lyme disease.

After a few weeks Andy and I finally had sex. Up until then we had said we were dating but pretty much continued acting like we had the whole time we'd been friends. But one night at his place, we drunkenly decided to consummate our newfound love.

It was terrible.

We made it through the whole thing without laughing, but the rest of it was awkward. At one point, when he was fumbling to make his penis connect with my vagina, I started to wonder if he was a virgin. No, he and Caryn had definitely had sex. I had heard it through the bedroom wall one night while I spent an hour in tears digging through my closet for earmuffs. It wasn't that he didn't know how to do it; we just didn't know how to do it with each other. I wrote it off as nerves. It felt like we had an assignment to complete and we just wanted to turn it in and see what kind of grade we got. Maybe there was a reason that we'd been able to sleep in the same bed for so many months and never fool around. Physical attraction was not what was driving us.

The next morning he barely looked at me. He acted uncomfortable and distant. I felt like I was going to throw up. I couldn't already be showing signs of pregnancy, so this meant I knew our relationship was over before it really started. I have no idea what went through his head, or why us finally having sex brought anything romantic between us to a screeching halt, but it didn't do much for my self-esteem. Even though I knew I didn't really enjoy it, I hated knowing that *he* didn't. I went home that morning and immediately called my friend Michele. She was one of my best friends in college, from my theater side.

Michele was a lot like me. We met when we were doing a play together. Early on in our friendship she had sex in a park with a guy she had just met and told me the next day she thought she had grass stains on her underwear. I instantly loved her. She was the first person that I connected with in the college/theater world that I felt comfortable bringing around my work friends.

"There's something wrong with my vagina," I said when Michele answered.

"Sarah?"

"Yeah, it's me. There's something wrong with my vagina."

"Okay. Do you need to go to the doctor?"

"No, not like that. It's something else. It scared Andy. My vagina scared Andy. We aren't going to be together anymore. We had sex and now he hates me. God, maybe it isn't normal-looking. What does yours look like?"

"It's nine A.M. It probably doesn't look good."

"I'm serious, Michele. Do you have innies or outies? One night of sex and Andy is done with me. We barely even did it. It was kind of quick and not at all romantic and now he won't look at me. I left and he barely said a word."

"Well, how did you feel about it? Did you enjoy it?"

"No, it was terrible. But I love him. It'll get better; it was just our first go at it. Shit, why is this happening? Oh, I know! I'll call you back!"

I hung up on her and dialed Logan's phone number. He and I had been friends since we were in high school. We had dated when we first met, then decided we were better as friends. We were the exact opposite of me and Andy. But Logan had seen my vagina. He could tell me what the problem was.

"Hello?" Logan answered, sounding sleepy.

"What's wrong with my vagina?" I asked.

"Sarah?"

"Yes, damnit. What the fuck is wrong with my vagina?"

"I have no idea what you are talking about."

I told him the story. He just sat there quiet. *Oh, God . . .* he knew he was going to have to tell me that I had a deformed vagina. He had hoped he'd never have to. Now he couldn't find the words.

"Logan? You have to tell me. We've been friends forever. You're a guy. What is going on?" The tears started pouring down my face.

Logan took a deep breath. "Sarah, it sounds like . . . well, it sounds like he got freaked out. Maybe it was too fast."

"Too fast? Too fucking fast? We've been friends for two years. We've spent so much time together. Usually I have sex right up front. How is this too *fast*?"

"Maybe it was too fast for you guys to move to that level. Maybe he just wants to stay friends."

My heart exploded. *Friends.* I had enough friends. "I have to go." I was choking on my own tears.

"Hey. For the record, you have a perfectly normal vagina. It's not attractive, but none of them are."

I hung up.

For a couple of days Andy and I just ignored each other. I couldn't understand how he could go so long without talking to me. I also couldn't understand how he could be so disrespectful. He knew he needed to call. As his best girlfriend, I'd told him a million times that he had to call girls. Now it was me who was on the other end of it. I was pissed. I couldn't call him; we were in a staring contest and I wasn't about to lose. We always said we were friends first. We had promised this wouldn't mess anything up and now it felt like it had.

In the midst of my anger I had answered my own question. He wasn't in love. He had just gotten wrapped up in the idea of it, but the second intimacy came into play he didn't feel what he'd hoped he'd feel. I knew because I'd done the same thing in the past, but unfortunately, this time I was the one left holding my heart in my hands.

I broke the silence with a phone call. I figured the only way to salvage this was to give him the rope he needed to get out of the hole he'd dug for himself. I didn't know how to not have him in my life. I decided I needed to make it okay for him so that I didn't totally lose him. Pretty pathetic, yes. But I was too invested and I figured if I played it cool now, we'd get back on track then maybe become wildly attracted to each other and give dating another shot. That's when I thought sex could get better over time. Too bad my thirty-six-year-old self couldn't have paid my nineteen-year-old self a visit then and told me that when sex is bad, it's bad. There's no changing it; you have to pick up your underwear and move on.

I assumed he wouldn't answer the phone, just as his best girlfriend had taught him to do when attempting to avoid a girl. I figured he'd tell Joby to take the call and pretend he wasn't there, but I would leave a message, which would open the lines of communication. I was surprised when he picked up on the first ring. Obviously he did not have caller ID.

"Hello?" he said.

"I was just reading this *Cosmo* quiz. How to tell if having sex with someone you are friends with has ruined—"

"I'm sorry," he said right away. "I really am."

"It's fine!" I shouted in a really exaggerated upbeat tone. "We're all good. That was totally weird. Let's not do *that* again. Gross! Oh, and I'm totally not reading *Cosmo* right now. That was just a hilarious joke."

Pause. "Oh, okay. You understand . . . ?"

"Look, it's obvious we should just be friends; that's what we are. Don't worry about it and let's not ever discuss it again!" I screamed.

"Okay. You sure it's all right? I feel kind of . . ."

"Like an asshole?"

Silence.

"I'm joking! You're not an asshole. I have to go to class, then I have a date later, so let's talk next week!"

"A date . . . ?"

"Yes. Why . . . are you jealous?"

"I don't know, I . . ."

"I'm kidding. But I do have to get to class!" I slammed down the phone. *That went really well,* I lied to myself. *Totally normal.*

Luckily the volume of my voice alerted all of my roommates to the situation and I didn't have to come out and retell my sob story. Instead they were just in the living room waiting to give me a big group hug. Thank God I lived with the sorority girls, because the theater girls usually smelled like patchouli. That hug at least smelled like a nice Yankee Candle.

I spent the next several weeks getting really intoxicated, even more than normal. I was trying to remember if I had ever felt that kind of pain before. I thought about Bucky. I thought about Rhonda Lewis and the hickey. I decided that this felt worse. I decided that when all of that happened I was a foolish kid. Now I was a nineteen-year-old woman and I could feel *real* feelings. I was feeling very dramatic. Thank God I was a drama major.

## ALCOHOL IS FOR CLOSURES

**H**aving my heart broken by Andy proved to be amazing for my sex life. In the theater department, the whole "dating the co-stars" thing isn't exaggerated. It's like what you hear about movie stars, but on a much more pathetic level. There was one exception: I was in a show called *The House of Bernarda Alba,* and I didn't hook up with anybody during that time. It was an all-female cast and I wasn't one of those "experimental" theater girls. If you've never heard of that show, it's a Spanish tragedy. It never occurred to any of us that it was ridiculous for eight girls with Southern accents to be wandering around whining about our lost love, Pepe el Romano.

Since I wasn't taking men seriously anymore, I developed a crush on a guy named Steven. He was younger than me, eighteen to my twenty. I usually dated guys at least a couple of years older than me, so I was feeling good about how much I was branching out. Steven was really, really cute and really, really interested in me. He was also a virgin. I became very interested in what it would be like to date someone who didn't have a sexual connection to anybody else but me. It seemed like that would make me really important.

Steven and I started hanging out after rehearsals for a show that we were in called *The American Clock*. He played a young guy and I played an aunt. It made making out a little creepy but I worked through it. There was something very empowering about being a couple of years older than him. I felt as if I were this wise older woman who came into his life to teach him the ways of the world. It was really helping me with my role, too. He, on the other hand, was just ready to ditch his virginity.

The sex itself wasn't so bad, but then again my standards were still low. It was at least better than with Andy. In college, sex is very rushed and things are pushed and twisted and you wake up wondering if your nipples will ever be the same. *Let's take this slow and find out what feels good* doesn't really start to happen until your late twenties. And that's only if you figure out that it's okay to ask for it. The bigger problem that I encountered with taking Steven's virginity was the overwhelming feeling of responsibility that followed.

Guys don't have that feeling of responsibility after sex; at least Bucky didn't. He was only interested in high-fiving the other morons in the locker room. That was not the case for me with Steven. The second we were finished, which was about two seconds after we started, I felt the weight of the world on my chest. Lying next to him, I started to panic.

*What am I supposed to do now? He probably wants to marry me. I'm not prepared for that kind of commitment. I'm moving to California the second I graduate. Successful actresses don't date guys who have only fucked one girl. This is a disaster.*

I quickly called it quits. I couldn't end things while we were still in the show, because I didn't want his performance to suffer. So the day after it closed, I asked him to meet me in the park. He rode up on his bike wearing a silly-looking newsboy cap. We sat on a bench and talked for a couple of hours. Within the first five minutes, I told him we could no longer date. He said it was okay, then I cried and rambled on for the next hour and fifty-five minutes while he patiently comforted me for breaking up with him.

"It's okay, Sarah, I understand. We can still be friends."

"Friends? Oh my God, you're so young and innocent! You can't be friends with someone that you're in love with! Believe me, I know."

"If you're in love with me, why are you breaking up with me?"

"*No,* you're in love with *me.*"

"Um, I just kind of thought—"

"I'm sorry, but this is the way it has to be," I interrupted. "I have to go." I walked away dramatically.

I usually find that if I end a relationship, I'm more devastated than if the other person ends it. If I make the decision not to be with someone, I'm closing the door on a future with them, but it's my choice. So if it's the wrong choice, that's on me. If *they* break things off with *me* then I don't have to feel responsible, and I don't have to question whether I just walked away from the perfect guy, since I wasn't the one doing the walking. Don't get me wrong; it still hurts but it's somehow more reassuring. I *had* broken up with Steven, but in this case I knew I wouldn't have any regrets.

The next play I was in was called *Bus Riley's Back in Town*. It's a play about a guy named Bus Riley who is back in town. My co-star was a guy named Nick. Nick liked to drink whiskey.

Nick lived with his girlfriend but he was miserable with her. Really everything made him miserable, but he covered it up with moments of what seemed like joy. I assumed that I could make him happy. I can't say for sure that he was manic-depressive, but I *can* say for sure that he reminded me a lot of my Uncle John, who was manic-depressive. John was someone who when I was younger I thought was one of the happiest people that I'd ever met. I later found out that my parents just didn't let me around him when he was having an "episode." When they did finally decide that I was old enough to be told that he was sick, I insisted on seeing him. My dad made arrangements and we paid Uncle John a visit in Sacramento. I was about thirteen and we met him at a diner. It felt like he didn't want us to see where he lived, which turned out to be the case because he didn't have a home. My grandma was secretly harboring him even though she'd been told over and over that she was enabling him; everyone else kept him at a distance since he refused to stay on his medication and get the help he so desperately needed. She didn't care. A woman that will take the bus cross-country to see her grandkids has a lot of dedication in her. And she was his mother.

John was really nervous when we all sat down in the big red booth; my dad had told him that my sister and I now knew about his condition. He tried to overcompensate with humor. When I asked him how he was doing, he said, "Just trying to stay away from the chain saws," and laughed.

I was, and still am, terrified of chain saws. I won't even set foot in a haunted house because I'm convinced that the person holding the chain saw is an actual serial killer using Halloween as their excuse to go nuts. All year they wait for the night they get to dress up and act like it's all fun and games, then when the moment is right people who just thought they were out for a good scare will get their heads sliced off. The movie *Halloween* really fucked me up. Uncle John's joke made my head spin.

The most attractive thing about Nick was that he was a complete mess *and* an adult. He started classes then dropped them. He wanted to be an actor but felt like he was too smart for it and should probably teach English. All of his noncommittal bullshit made me really horny.

After Andy, I didn't think I would ever fall in love again, but it was happening. Nick made me feel incredibly safe and incredibly insecure at the same time. There isn't anything more tempting than that combination. It's like someone offering you a grilled cheese and bacon sandwich right after you start a diet.

Nick flirted with me, but I couldn't decide if it was real flirting or if he was just researching his role of Bus Riley. He seemed to be taking his acting seriously during those few weeks, and I liked it. I was starting to find guys in my classes hotter than the guys from the fraternity houses. Frat guys were fun for a night, but brooding actor guys had me really interested, and Nick was an amazing brooder. It wasn't until my late twenties that I figured out the guys I had been labeling as brooding were probably just alcoholics.

One night after a long, emotional rehearsal where my character agonized over the return of Bus Riley, Nick and I decided to go for a drink. We were physically exhausted from what our characters were going through. We decided that a pitcher of beer at Fuzzy's was the perfect way to unwind. As a bonus, Max was working that night. He was too dumb to figure out that since I never returned any of his calls he should start charging me for drinks.

One free pitcher led to another, and the next thing I knew Nick and I were in my shitty Mustang on our way to the same place Andy and I had gone the night we decided to give "us" a try. I guess my car just knew that when it was time for me to break the make-out ice with someone, it should head to the park. We pulled over, parked discreetly underneath a giant lamppost, and shoved our tongues into each other's mouths.

It didn't take long for a cop to pound on the window. I put my shirt back on and asked him what I could do for him.

"You can get out your ID and step out of the car, that's what you can do for me."

I obliged, but in the back of my mind I was trying to figure out how the hell I could keep from getting arrested.

Luckily I was an actress; the tears immediately started streaming down my face. I began telling the cop all about the huge fight Nick and I had just had.

"We've been together since I was fifteen!" I told the cop. "A few months ago I found out that he cheated on me and we broke up. He felt so bad. You know, like when you screw up and then you realize that person was the best thing that has ever happened to you? Like that song 'Don't Know What You've Got (Till It's Gone)' by Cinderella. That's what happened with us. So now we're making up. Do you think I'm making a mistake?"

"I don't know. I mean, sometimes guys screw up, you have to consider—wait, what are you two doing at the park this late?"

"This is our spot! It's where we first kissed. He wanted to come here to make up, like a fresh start. Isn't that romantic?" The tears were flowing. I was so excited that I could cry on cue that I almost forgot to focus on my lie.

The cop let us go home with a warning. He told me to get home safe and "be careful with my heart." I was in college. I didn't listen to cops.

Nick and I kept seeing each other for a while. He and his girlfriend eventually broke up, most likely because I dropped him off at 4 A.M. several nights a week. At the time I was sure that hearts had to be followed—no matter the circumstances. That's what the girl who walked down the aisle throwing rose petals at her dad's wedding only months after her family fell apart believed. That was just the way things worked. The other side of me, the grown-up girl who believes in commitment, now knows that during that time I was a selfish asshole and so was Nick.

Nick decided that I was now his girlfriend and we continued to be really fond of each other during play rehearsals. My feelings for him intensified my character's joy that Bus Riley was back in town. People started saying that I was a really good actress. Co-star dating was great for my career.

When Nick and I would go out, we'd get drunk. He liked to drink whiskey and smoke cigarettes. I was already on board with the whiskey, so I just needed to take up smok-

ing again. I had smoked a little in high school, which traced
back to Austin Cooper. Austin had ridiculous dimples and
looked amazing in a pair of Wranglers. I don't care what
you say, the Arkansas girl in me will always find that look
attractive. With him I had discovered that if you were talking to a guy and he wanted a cigarette, the best way to get
some one-on-one time with him was to also want a cigarette. This can even apply to female friends, but the payoff
isn't as rewarding. Nick actually reminded me a lot of Austin,
without the Southern accent. Nick was from Virginia and
liked to read Jack Kerouac. Austin was from Prairie Grove
and couldn't read. Austin smoked Marlboro Reds, so my
throat suffered more than my heart did when he broke it.
He's been arrested a few times in the past couple of years for
something to do with meth. Just like Garth Brooks said,
sometimes it's good when things don't work out with somebody you think you love.

While Nick and I were dating, my roommates graduated
and I had to find a new place to live. I moved in with these
girls Amanda and Heather from my acting classes. Amanda
was a big lesbian. Lesbians loved me in college. Flattering at
the time, but in retrospect that was probably less about me
and more about my haircut.

Amanda and Heather had been friends for years and I
really liked them. I was excited that my new roommate
situation would be as fun as my previous one. Heather and
Nick were also close, maybe a little too close. I can't say for
sure if anything ever happened between them, but it seemed
like something had happened between them. At first I attrib-
uted their bond to their similar moodiness. Heather used
to lock herself in her room, light candles, and cry, while
Amanda and I sat in the living room playing the drinking

game Quarters. Heather also wandered into the kitchen at night and would guzzle an entire carton of milk. Then she'd claim that she didn't remember doing it, blaming it on "sleepwalking." I'm sure she has incredibly strong bones now, but the whole time I lived with her I had to eat dry Cocoa Puffs.

Shortly after moving into our new place, we decided to have a party. Nick had been acting strange, and I was pretty sure I needed to break up with him. He'd been blowing off school and was starting to seem really irresponsible. My mom has always scared me into believing that if I pay my gas bill one hour late I will never be able to get a home loan, so I can be a bit uptight. The things I had loved most about Nick were that he had similar interests as me, and had aspects of being responsible, but was still fun. I've found throughout my life that that is a hard combination to find: Guys tend to be one or the other, but rarely both. Now that the responsible side of him seemed to be fading, I was getting sick of his brooding. I got enough of that living with Heather. I just wanted a roommate who would twirl broomsticks again and a boyfriend who finished his classes. The night of the party, he couldn't keep it together. He was drunk and rambling, then he went outside, set a bush on fire, and brought it into the house. It was a direct slap in the face to my fire department roots.

I was pretty sure he was in a blackout at the party so I decided to wait until the morning to tell him that it was over between us. I explained that we were just going in "different directions," which I'd heard someone use as an excuse to leave a woman with amnesia on *General Hospital*.

About three weeks later, Nick announced that he was

moving back to Virginia. He told me he didn't want to lose contact with me, and promised that he would write. I liked the idea of a guy writing me letters. It seemed really romantic. For a while I got a letter every week. He claimed to write them while he was on his porch drinking his whiskey and smoking cigarettes and he referred to himself as a poet. I don't know what the deal is with me and guys that I break up with deciding to write poems to me, but at least Nick's were legible and he didn't make up words like Bucky did. He also never called me his "ho" in any of them. My standards had risen.

I was still having fun living with Amanda. She was great at being a lesbian—she brought home lots of girls. But one night I pulled into the driveway and caught her making out with this guy Rob in his car, which was confusing for me. I didn't want her to fuck things up. Having a lesbian roommate made me feel really open-minded for a girl who grew up in a town with one thousand people. She apologized for making out with a guy and assured me that she was really a lesbian.

"I was drunk. I didn't know what I was doing."

"It's okay," I comforted her. "Just don't let it happen again."

Eventually Heather decided to move to another state. I would miss her but was excited to finally be able to keep a carton of milk in the house. Now we needed a replacement roommate. Amanda asked her friend Misty, who was also a lesbian, to move in. Now I was a straight girl living with two lesbians. I could see my sitcom developing and I hadn't even moved to California yet.

Unfortunately Misty was out of her mind. She used to

write mean things about Amanda and me on pieces of paper then leave them in odd places. I'd lift up a Q-tip box or a plant and read that I lived like a pig and had fat arms. I was very clean and prided myself on it, so the living like a pig part really pissed me off. Each time Amanda or I found a passive-aggressive note, Misty would act surprised and say that she didn't write it. It made no sense. If she didn't want us to find them, she'd have thrown them away. She was like a mean note hoarder. I do think if she would have lived there for much longer she would have killed me. Amanda and I had daily meetings, trying to figure out how to ask Misty to leave without incident. Luckily one day we came home and she was just gone. She'd taken all of her stuff. Angry notes were left uncovered everywhere. She really hated us. I guess she couldn't take me or my fat arms anymore. I was relieved that she had left without murdering me in my sleep, but now Amanda and I needed a third roommate yet again.

A week later, Nick wrote me one of his drunken letters and told me he was coming back to finish school. Amanda thought this was the perfect situation—he could just move in with us. I was hesitant. I was over him at that point, but I hated his mood swings. Those are only fun when you really like someone. I wasn't quite comfortable with the idea of him being our roommate. So he moved in.

He and Amanda had sex a few times, which was pretty confusing. I didn't even really care that she and I had had sex with the same guy who was now living with us; I just cared that she was a lesbian. I was sure we had talked about this behavior when she made out with Rob. I asked her to stop having sex with Nick, which surprised her because she didn't think I knew about it.

"You guys are my roommates. Of course I know."

"I'm sorry. Are you upset? I thought you didn't have feelings for him anymore."

"I don't. I don't think I do anyway. It's just weird, mostly because you're a lesbian. It feels like you're losing focus. You're in COLLEGE! This is the time of your life to be a lesbian."

"I know. You're right. I don't even like guys. Sometimes I just slip up," she explained.

"Okay. Just don't let it happen again. I can't lose another friend."

"What are you talking about?"

"What are *you* talking about?" I asked back. I knew I was talking about Andy, but I didn't know if *she* knew I was talking about Andy. I also didn't feel like crying.

"No, I mean when you said you can't lose another friend. Who are you talking about?"

"What?"

"This game sucks," Amanda conceded.

"Who do you think, Amanda?" Tears started to stream down my face, but they weren't the kind I mustered up on cue. "Andy. I lost Andy. And now we barely hang out and when we do we both act like fucking morons. It's so dumb."

Amanda hugged me. I wept like a baby. If I'm even kind of upset and then someone hugs me, I lose my shit.

Fuck. It was my senior year and my heart still belonged to Andy. I didn't understand what the problem was. I'd had a few boyfriends since, even ones that I really had feelings for, like Nick. But somehow, no matter what, my heart still skipped ten beats when I was around Andy, even though those times were few and far between.

A couple of weeks later Andy asked me to meet him for lunch. I was usually the one who instigated us getting together, so I was particularly excited at his invitation. I put on my lucky toe ring and did the best I could with my hair.

Andy wasn't much for small talk, so he got to the point right after the chips and queso arrived.

"I'm moving to Little Rock."

I stared at him. Little Rock was four hours away, probably fourteen hours in my Mustang.

"That's really exciting," I lied. "What are you going to do there?" I felt the tears coming up and fought them with everything that I had. *Not here,* I thought. *Not at Chili's.*

"I'm not sure. I just need a change . . . are you okay?"

"I'm great! This queso is just so spicy." My face does sweat when I eat spicy food, so it wasn't a total lie.

"Are you sure?"

"Oh, shit. I forgot I have a test in an hour!"

"But it's Saturday."

"I know! Rude, right? I'll see you later."

I bolted home, into my room, and cried into my pillow, hoping not to stir the neighbors. Any hope that I had in the back of my mind that we would end up together had just fizzled. I knew that I was planning on moving away, but I wanted to leave first. I didn't want him to leave me. Suddenly it didn't feel easier to have someone make the final decision for me. That previous theory was so stupid. This was so much worse. I wondered if this was how my mom felt when my dad made the decision for them.

I guess I cried myself to sleep because the next thing I knew, Nick was sitting on the side of my bed rubbing my back.

"Are you okay?" he asked.

I rolled over and looked at him. "I'm fine. Why?"

"Well, I got home a little while ago and it sounded like

you were playing one of those whale sounds CDs in your room, but I know your CD player is broken. What's up?"

I was taken aback by his concern. Even though we were roommates I hadn't felt the friendship that we had once shared. I had really distanced myself from him. I'd let him move in after a long discussion about how I didn't want it to be weird between us and I assumed he understood part of it "not being weird" was not fucking our lesbian roommate.

The Nick I used to love was back, if only for that afternoon. He comforted me. He spoke about Andy and me in ways that confused me, because they hadn't spent much time together.

"How do you know so much about this?"

"You love him," he said to me.

"Why do you think that? Why do you know that? I'm supposed to be over him, and you're all supposed to think that. Oh God, do you think that he knows . . . ?"

"I just know what you look like when you're in love."

I released a sound so horrible I'm not even sure it classifies as a cry. It shocked me to the point that I began to laugh. Nick started to laugh, too. It was just like old times—so we had sex.

That afternoon's festivities were like the breakup sex that we never had; neither of us took it seriously. The only thing that really stuck with me was that he encouraged me to tell Andy how I felt before it was too late.

I didn't listen to Nick. I figured since he was someone who should probably be on medication he wasn't necessarily the best person to take advice from. But as I was approaching my senior year, I decided I wanted to check out a theater company in Little Rock. At least that's why I told Andy I was going to be in his neighborhood.

Andy offered to let me stay on his couch. My plan was to stay on his face. I didn't want to leave Arkansas without getting this sex thing right with him.

When I got to his apartment, everything felt weird. There was more distance between us than before. I didn't take this as a hint; in fact I took it the opposite. Here's the psychotherapy rundown of it all: If you grow up fighting for a man's attention, specifically your father, you will probably find yourself attracted to men whose attention you have to fight for. I also realize this is not exactly groundbreaking information.

That night in Little Rock, Andy and I had sex on a pull-out couch in his apartment. It was even more awkward than the first time we did it. We just went through the motions and neither of us seemed to be getting any real enjoyment from it. It was blatantly clear that we would never have sexual chemistry. With him I really wanted to let it slide. I guess I thought there was something more, but thank God we never worked out because I really do like sex and that kind of relationship would have been a huge bummer. When we were finished, Andy didn't stay on the bed with me nor did he invite me to his room. He just went to his bedroom and left me on the couch with my own thoughts, which were mainly focused on not crying so hard that the police would show up.

The next morning I woke up before him, so I left. I drove home and decided to put him out of my mind and focus on enjoying my last few months in not only college, but in Arkansas. I was involved in something called the "Mount Sequoyah New Play Retreat" and it was about to start. Mount Sequoyah is a beautiful place on the top of a mountain, with tons of cabins and a beautiful view. It seemed like a good way to go out.

The retreat was for playwrights to come and workshop their new shows. The actors would work with them, then at the end we'd put the shows up for an audience. A few of my friends from theater, including Michele, were also doing it. There were some others whom I hadn't met who used to go to the University of Arkansas and were coming back to participate. One of those guys, John, was really cute. Michele laid dibs on him pretty quickly and followed through. They were making out within about two hours of meeting, and it was the middle of the day.

It was my last few weeks in Fayetteville. Since Michele had taken up with John, there weren't a ton of options for distracting myself from thoughts of Andy. I tried not to care, but at night after rehearsals it became kind of a bummer that I didn't have a make-out partner. We'd all go out for drinks, but I just didn't find any of the new guys interesting, although there *was* one who thought he was really suave. His name was Colin. He had gone to school at the U of A and was now living in California. From what I heard, when he was at the U of A he fucked everybody. He was kind of cute, but his sleazy attitude that he could get any woman he wanted was really annoying. He constantly tried to flirt with me, but I laughed him off.

The thing about guys who act like that is that eventually I wind up attracted to them. At first I find them ridiculous, then I feel sorry for them, then I develop a crush. The final night of the retreat, I put my favorite long, wavy crinkle skirt over my black bodysuit, added my favorite choker for good luck, and headed out to party.

The more I drank that night, the more Colin's behavior became irresistible to me. I walked over to Michele and told her that I was going to hook up with him that night. I wanted her permission.

"Really? I knew it! I say go for it. He's totally cute," she encouraged.

"He is, right? Did you know that he was in *Biloxi Blues*?"

"Really? That Matthew Broderick movie?"

"Yep. They filmed some of it here or something. Whatever—Andy's never been in a movie." With that I sauntered off toward Colin to laugh at his dumb jokes all night long. He was eating it up.

I can't tell you the specifics of the rest of that night because I don't remember them. All I know is that I woke up in my bed and my clothes were not on. My head was pounding. I stood up to go get some water and aspirin, then caught a glimpse of myself in the mirror. I was still wearing one part of my outfit. Naked with a choker: not a good look. I then saw a note on my dresser.

"Had so much fun. I'm headed back to CA today. Love, C."

Gross. He called himself "C." It wouldn't have taken him that long to add the other four letters. Even grosser— he'd left me a note. I knew he was going back to California that day; I didn't need a Post-it to remind me. I had intended that night to be a one-night stand and now he'd gone and trumped me with a note; God he was full of himself. If he was still there I would have fucked him again just so I could get the last word in. I slowly stumbled back to my bed and called Michele.

"Hello?" she answered groggily.

"I woke up wearing nothing but a choker," I told her.

"That sounds dangerous."

"It is not a good look," I warned her.

"Is he still there?"

"No. But he left a note."

"Gross. Does your head hurt?"

"Yes. Is John still there?"

"No, he left. Want to go get a Bloody Mary?"

"Yes."

We met at our favorite place, the Grill, and drank for the entire afternoon. She asked about the night with Colin, but I didn't remember any of the details.

"I just know we used a condom. I found the wrapper. So there's that."

"Oh that's too bad. He would have made a great father."

"I hope I never sober up again," I stated. Then I polished off another drink.

A couple of weeks later, some friends from work decided to have a going-away party for me at their place. I was just about to graduate and I was going through with my plans to move to California to make my living as an actress and a comedian. I wondered if I should have two different parties, one with my friends from classes and one with my friends from work. But then I figured, screw it. I was about to leave anyway. Having all of the people I loved under one roof just might be a blast.

The party was exactly what I expected it to be. Everyone was drinking and I did a lot of crying. I couldn't believe that I was about to move. I'd been in Arkansas for most of my life. I didn't know how I was going to pull it off.

Andy's appearance was a surprise. Nobody had warned me. I was happy to see him, but at the same time I wished he would have stayed in Little Rock, or perhaps jumped off a cliff. We hadn't even talked since he'd pulled out on his pull-out.

With the exception of the time I ordered all of Olivia Newton-John's records on Amazon, I've never made a great decision while intoxicated. The night of that party was no exception. Everything was going fine—I felt loved and supported and special. The only thing that kept bothering me was the situation with Andy. I didn't like that we were going to say goodbye at this party, possibly forever, without discussing what had happened between us. I just wanted to say something, get some *closure*.

If you are a girl, you probably know that *closure* is the excuse that most of us use to do something dramatic. Saying you are doing something for *closure* is just covering up your one last futile attempt to tell someone how you feel in hopes that they will come around to admit that they feel the same way about you and the two of you will ride off into the sunset leaving all of your cares behind. So, I went to find Andy in order to get *closure*.

I don't know if you've ever had forty drinks and then spilled your guts to someone, but I don't recommend it. We stood there for an awkward moment, and then I unleashed. I told him that I had been in love with him for years. I told him that even when he was with Caryn I was in love with him. I told him that no matter who I was with, he was the one who I wished I was with. I told him that he was my best friend and how often does a woman get to fall in love with her best friend? I told him everything.

"But you're moving away," was his response.

I stared at him. No fucking kidding I was moving away.

That's why I was standing on a lawn after drinking a gallon of Jack Daniel's telling him that I loved him.

"That's your response?" I asked.

"Well, you're leaving, right?"

"Yes," I slurred. "What are you getting at?"

He just looked at me. His eyes said it all. Mine probably said, "I'm seconds away from alcohol poisoning."

I guess in my heart I knew what he wanted to say. It was a weird time for me to lay all of my cards out on the table. I shouldn't have even bothered to put myself through it. If he'd returned my feelings, it wasn't going to change my plans. Maybe I'd hoped he'd come with me. I didn't know. I just knew that now I had closure. It felt anything but great. Fuck *closure*.

# CABO WOBBLE

**M**y post-college plan was to stay with my dad in Orange County, get a job as a waitress, save enough money to get an apartment, and move to L.A. I hadn't spent much time with my father over the last four years. Once I started in college, I quit visiting him for the summer. Moving in with him was going to be weird.

To prep myself I went to visit him for my senior year spring break. I figured I needed to spend a little time to 1) make sure we still got along and 2) meet my new stepmom, Shirley. She's my third stepmom, with a couple of broken-off engagements in between. She's the one that stuck. My dad had quit the newspaper business and was attempting to start a wine club, which meant that I got to spend my spring break wine tasting in a beautiful place in California called Paso Robles. Not a bad deal for a twenty-one-year-old.

Shirley and I got along great. I've since watched her throw a drink in a twenty-two-year-old girl's face for calling her an "old bitch." She's pretty fantastic. While Dad and his best friend, Joe, were off having meetings at wineries, Shirley and I went to sample the wines with Joe's wife, Marsha. We got hammered. She was even fine with me stealing glasses from the wineries that wouldn't let me keep the glass. *This is great!*

I was relieved that I liked Shirley so much. It was going to be interesting enough living with my dad again; I didn't want to have issues with her on top of it. They'd only been married for a couple of months when I got there so I'm sure *she* was thrilled that her new husband's twenty-one-year-old daughter was moving in with them.

I drove out to California with Logan and two other work friends. We all crammed into my Mustang with a U-Haul trailer attached to the back. When we pulled out of my mother's driveway, she cried and waved, I cried and waved. It was very dramatic.

It was also the end of June. The drive across country in hundred-degree weather was a fucking disaster. Yes, I had air-conditioning in my car. No, it did not work well. We all hated one another by the end of the trip.

Our pit stop in Vegas turned out to be a few days longer than originally planned; none of us wanted to get back in that piece of shit car. I won a hundred dollars on blackjack, which I spent one morning on McDonald's breakfast. I was hungover. I ordered a lot.

We arrived in California the week of July fourth. Joe

and Marsha decided that they would have a little "welcome" party for me at their house. They had a lovely pool, a nice backyard, and a gorgeous son named Anthony. When I met him, I thought they were pulling some sort of prank on me. I couldn't believe that my dad's best friend had a hot Italian son close to my age. I immediately began planning our wedding.

Anthony was a cop. He had a cop body and cop testosterone. It was a little jarring at first. I was used to guys who ran around in tights rehearsing lines and dumb frat guys who ran around in Tommy Hilfigers doing bong hits. But if this was what California had to offer I was okay with it. I have a real thing for Italian guys. Aside from my baseball wife dream, I have a weird fantasy of being married to the mob, but not really like Henry Hill in *GoodFellas*. That's too depressing. Somewhere more in between Tony Soprano and Sonny from *General Hospital*. I've also always been pretty horny for Andy Garcia. I know that he's Cuban, but I can't tell the difference.

At one point during the party we ran out of beer. Anthony offered to go get some more and asked if I'd like to join him. I followed him out to the driveway. We got into his truck and then I asked: "Are you okay to drive? We've been drinking all day."

"I'm a cop!" he said excitedly and started the engine.

When we left, he kept the window down, then reached out to pull the garage door closed while he backed out, moving quickly so that the door just missed the hood of his truck. He could've just used the automatic garage door opener, but that's the testosterone thing that I was talking about. Nothing really happened during the ride, but at the time it was the best half hour of my life. I felt like I was really going to like California.

Back at the party, Anthony asked if I wanted to take a quick ride on his (wait for it) motorcycle. Now he wasn't just a hot guy, he was a hot guy with a motorcycle. God had really taken his time when putting this man together. While we went for a little spin around the block on his motorcycle, I imagined what it would be like on our wedding day when we pulled out of the church on his bike. My white dress would be flowing and we'd wave goodbye to our friends and family as all of his cop buddies fired their guns in the air. I have no idea if cops do that at a wedding, but they would do it at ours. Our families would stand together, laughing and crying.

"I can't believe that my daughter married my best friend's son," my dad would say through tears of joy. "This is perfect."

When we got back to the house, I climbed off and immediately felt pain shoot through my leg. I was a little drunk, so the pain wasn't as bad as it could have been; sometimes alcohol comes in handy. I looked down and realized I had burned my leg on the motorcycle exhaust pipe.

"Shit, I told you to be careful around that!" Anthony ran and ripped open an aloe plant from the yard (I thought, *People have aloe plants in their yards here?*), broke it in half, and dripped the aloe onto my new wound. Any pain that subsided had nothing to do with the plant. It had to do with the hot Italian guy standing over me tending to my injury.

Later that afternoon Shirley told me that I was going to need eyelid surgery. She said that if I looked closely at my dad, I would notice that his eyelids are really droopy.

"By the time he's eighty he probably won't even be able to see."

"Oh," I replied. "What does that have to do with me?"

"You have your father's eyelids. They already droop a little. It's only going to get worse as you get older. You're twenty-one: That's the perfect age to take care of it. Insurance will probably cover it."

Great. I had just moved to California and I already needed plastic surgery. I hoped that Anthony wasn't turned off by my fucked-up eyelids.

After being in California for about two weeks, I found a bartending job close to my dad's house. I couldn't wait to start making some money. I mean, I was fresh out of school and living with my dad for the first time since I was five years old . . . and he had just gotten married. Everyone involved wanted me in and out of that house as quickly as possible.

When I got off from work my co-workers and I always went out to T.G.I. Friday's. It was not the club scene that I assumed I'd see when I moved to California; it was that strip mall/chain restaurant mentality that I was familiar with from Arkansas. It made me comfortable and every once in a while I'd feel like I was still back home. The people I worked with were fun and I had officially made my first California friends. The only problem was that all the houses on my father's street looked the same so more times than I can count I pulled into the wrong driveway only to discover my key didn't fit in the lock. "I just finished college . . . it was exhausting" was my constant excuse for drinking and sleeping in. I was actually just depressed because I'd left home, but I didn't figure that out until later.

Living with my father was when I really began to understand where my conflicting desires in life came from. Most of my life, my dad had a lot of money. When I moved in with him, and when he was trying to start his own business, that had changed. He was basically starting over—a new career, a new wife. It was odd to see, but he was struggling. He worried about money, which he'd never done before. He was still really fun, but something about him was different. I think losing the power he once had in his career humbled him, but as I know him now, I have to say it was good for him. It made him appreciate more the things that can't be bought. That being said, he's always loved to go out for drinks. When I was living with him he still let himself go out and have a lot of fun, regardless of the struggles. He was the exact opposite of my mother, and so was half of me.

My plans to marry Anthony were not panning out. So far all I'd gotten from him was a scar on my leg from the motorcycle burn. We'd only hung out a few more times since the party, and it didn't seem like it was leading to anything else. I figured it was for the best; I didn't need to get tied up in some messy relationship before I moved to L.A. It was like an hour-and-a-half drive and for that I'd at least need to be getting laid.

A few months later, I went on a weekend trip to Cabo San Lucas with one of the girls I worked with, Danielle. If you've never been to Cabo, just know that it's a mess. The bars are full of people doing shots and falling down. They play loud techno music everywhere you go. You can't sit at a table without some man or woman coming up to pour tequila down your throat and then shaking your head back and forth while blowing a whistle. It's awesome.

The first night that we were there we went to a bar called Cabo Wabo. Sammy Hagar owned it and rumor had it he was playing there that night. Danielle and I got as cute as possible and headed out for the evening. We started off at some weird street-corner taco stand that served tequila, then hit the local hot spots. By the time we got to Cabo Wabo, it was much later than we had anticipated and I was much drunker than necessary. We walked in just in time to hear Sammy Hagar say, "Good night, Cabo!" and exit the stage. Perfect timing, as always.

I woke up the next morning on the bathroom floor of the condo that we were staying in. My head was on a towel and I was curled up in the fetal position. I quickly noticed that I was fully clothed, and felt relieved. The last thing I remembered was Sammy Hagar saying good night. I had no idea how I ended up back there, alone on the bathroom floor. I wandered into Danielle's room to find out what the fuck had happened.

Danielle was asleep on her face. I poked her in the back a few times and she rolled over. She immediately started laughing.

"How was the bathroom floor?"

"Super comfortable. I don't know why I would bother with a bed. What the hell happened?"

"I have no idea. You said you were going to the bathroom at Cabo Wabo, then I never saw you again. I stayed out for a while and when I got back you were passed out on the bathroom floor. I tried to wake you—it wasn't happening."

There was no way I could have walked back; we were a few miles from the town and since I had no idea where I was I would have definitely gotten lost or kidnapped. I still don't know what happened. I've considered getting hypnotized to find out, but I don't really want to know.

"Let's go get a drink," I suggested.

"You're my hero," Danielle replied, and off we went to the pool bar.

While we were in Cabo we met a couple of cute boys from Quebec City who were ski instructors. They also loved to surf and told us that they came to Cabo every year to do just that. Both of them spoke French and their English was mediocre at best. Jackpot. The first night we met, one of them and I wound up in the pool at our complex, naked and confessing our feelings for each other. I had landed a French Canadian boyfriend named Marc for the remainder of the trip.

We had gotten to Cabo flying standby on some buddy passes. Don't ever do that. We got stuck there for three extra days, waiting to get on a flight. We'd also been staying for free in that condo because it was owned by a friend of a friend I knew from bartending. So for the unexpected extra days it was occupied by other vacationers and we had to scrape together money for a hotel. We didn't have much and winded up staying in a place so small that the toilet was in the shower.

When I finally knew I was getting on a plane, I called my dad to let him know what time to pick me up at the airport.

"Sorry, sweetie. Shirley and I are both busy tonight. Just grab a shuttle or even a cab. It won't cost much," he assured me.

Even though I only had seventeen dollars in my checking account at that point, it wasn't the cost that bothered me. It was the fact that I didn't have anybody picking me up at the airport. Family was supposed to pick you up; at least that's how we did it in Arkansas. It was something that I was used to and now that I'd moved to California yet another thing had changed. The adult me now knows, get your own ride to the airport. Getting to and from the airport in Los Angeles is much different than in Arkansas, and it isn't worth the hassle. If you're reading this, which you better be, sorry I didn't know that then, Dad.

When I finally got to Dad and Shirley's I went straight to bed. The next morning they were both acting not only normal, but super happy, so I decided to let the airport thing go. I didn't have many people to hang out with so I figured alienating them was not in my best interest. Instead I told them all about my trip and how much fun it was. I left out some details that most daughters should leave out—like how I had put myself in the position of getting date-raped by a Mexican cabdriver, and couldn't say with complete confidence that I hadn't been.

Surprisingly, Marc and I stayed in touch after the trip. He emailed me in broken English and I attempted to write at least one sentence in French with each response. I always had my English-to-French dictionary next to me when composing an email to him. It was fun to have a long-distance romance, especially since all I was doing in California so far was sleeping late and serving chicken wings.

Eventually Marc decided that he and I needed to see each other again. He invited me to come and stay with him in Quebec for a few days. He told me he wanted to fly me there and that the trip would cost me nothing. It took me about four seconds to agree to go.

When I told my dad that I was going, he was confused.

"How can you afford to go to Quebec?" he challenged.

"Marc is paying for everything!" I explained, excited.

Shirley was not confused—she was thrilled. She loved

the whole story: I'd met a hot guy on vacation, we were still talking, he wanted to fly me out to visit him.

"This is so romantic. You're going to have a great time!"

"Slow down, Shirley," my dad warned her. "Why would a guy pay for some girl who he just met . . ."

It hit him. He looked somewhere in between proud and horrified.

"I have a conference call," he mumbled and quickly exited the room.

I didn't stop him and ask him why he had a conference call since he was still unemployed.

During the flight to Quebec, I was nervous. I'd never done anything like that before. In fact, it was really out of character for me. Although I have done a lot of things that probably seem irresponsible to most people, I didn't and still don't tend to make big moves without agonizing over it for days. For once, I had just decided to go for it. I liked Marc, he liked me, and I felt like that was all I really needed to know.

I had made some good friends over my first few months in California, but I was still lonely. I thought perhaps Marc was exactly what I needed. He was a ski instructor and I had no idea how to ski. I had an opportunity to learn something from him. I didn't want to miss a real chance at an adventure— *that* would have been irresponsible.

Marc greeted me at the airport with a huge smile and two great biceps. He was even cuter than I remembered. He even surprised me with his English. I could instantly tell he'd been working on it.

"Have you been learning your French?" he asked.

"Yes!" I lied, hoping he wouldn't test me.

He then said something in French.

"Learning it and hearing it out loud are two different things," I explained. "Let's just speak English."

"Okay," he agreed. God he was cute.

I stared out the window the whole drive to his apartment.

"It's beautiful here." I smiled.

"In French we say—"

"I said we're speaking English, remember?"

His apartment was great, which was a relief. Most important, it was clean. I don't want to date a guy I'm going to have to clean up after. His place was also well decorated and really cozy. I did notice one big problem and started to panic: There was only one bathroom and it was smack in between the bedroom and the living room. This offered very little privacy. No way was I going to risk going number two in Marc's apartment and getting caught. It took me until I was thirty-four to live with somebody and even then I insisted on two bathrooms and zero discussion about what went on in them. Maybe that sounds weird coming from a girl who likes whiskey and baseball, but people have their lines and that is where I draw mine. I had to figure something out.

We spent the next few days going to long lunches, meeting his friends, and going out for drinks at night. Every place that we went, the first thing that I would do was go to the bathroom. After about my fifth time doing this, I returned to the table to find Marc smirking.

"You wan nex time I go with ewe?"

"What? Where?"

"I get it you go every time. I didn see the hint but now I see."

He thought I had some weird fascination with public bathrooms.

"No, I don't want to have sex in the bathroom. I'm just . . ."

He was still smiling.

"Sure, next time meet me there. I'd really love to have sex with you in a public bathroom," I lied. It was better than the truth. Now I'd just never be able to go to the bathroom again, ever, unless I was prepared to fuck him afterward.

Marc was funny and charming and his friends were just as great. They all found me extremely entertaining, which was a huge bonus. Toward the end of the week, we were going to a party on a big boat. Marc said they had one every year, and that all his friends would be there. Actually he may have said they had one every month—he still got most of his words mixed up. He also just kind of threw in that his mother would be at the party and wanted to know if that was okay with me.

"I guess it has to be okay because it sounds like she's coming!" I shouted.

"Well . . . if you dew noh wan my mom to comin is okay," he assured me.

"No, I don't really care for a Mountain Dew but as far as your mother goes I just said it was fine!"

He may not have spoken English but he did speak freaked-out woman. He tried his best to make me feel comfortable while I tried my best to figure out why I was so panicked. Sure, for the past few days I had been envisioning what our lives together would be like, but that was for me to do in my *head*. The second he started showing signs of actual commitment I became my father's daughter.

"I can't wait to meet her," I lied. "Is the fucking bar open yet?"

Despite my irrational fear of Marc's mother, the boat party turned out to be a lot of fun. I really liked the people that he surrounded himself with. Now all I had to get through was meeting his mom. I wasn't sure what I was so ramped up about; it was just somebody's mom. I loved moms! In fact the only mom I've ever really clashed with was my friend Casey's mom, who within three minutes of meeting me insisted that if I was single I must have been molested. And at this point I hadn't even met *her*. That would be five years down the road. I needed to calm down. *Where did I leave my drink?*

When she approached, I saw myself through her eyes. *There is the little slut that my lovely son met in that godforsaken Mexico. I can't believe he spent the money to fly the tramp all of the way here.* I knew that was what she was thinking, except in French.

Her name was Lynn and she could not have been nicer to me. She was doing an excellent job of hiding her disdain. She was the only person over thirty there and she didn't stay long, which led me to believe that she had made a special trip just to meet me, which led me to believe that Marc had asked her to, which led me to believe he was taking things too fast. After his mom left, he asked me how he should introduce me to people for the rest of the night.

"What do you mean? I always go by Sarah," I replied, clueless.

"I know. But when peeples ask who are you whut should I said?"

"It's not 'said,' it's . . . 'say.' "

"Okay, then what should I said?"

"It's . . . forget it. When people ask who I am, just say that I'm Sarah, because I am."

"I know but who should I said you are? Should I said that you are my geerlfrien?"

*Geerlfrien.* The word caught me off guard, but in a good way. I could be a girlfriend. I hadn't done it in a while, but I knew for sure I was good at it. I'd been told that in the past. I also liked being one. Plus it sounded so cute when he said it.

"Yes, you should definitely said that I'm your *geerlfrien,*" I said with a huge smile.

The rest of the night Marc and I were an official couple and I was enjoying it. We got really drunk, danced, and laughed. At the end of the night he insisted that we go eat *poutine,* which is basically the French version of getting your potatoes "smothered and covered" at the Waffle House. Thank God my new boyfriend liked late-night fast food as much as I did. We polished off four plates of it, then stumbled home to bed.

My last morning there I woke up and desperately needed to go to the bathroom. It might have been nerves, or it might have just been what a normal person does in the morning after four plates of *poutine.* Either way, I wasn't going to be able to wait until we went out for lunch to make my move. Marc cuddled up to me and I thought I was going to die. This was not the time to spoon.

"I'm starving," I told him.

"Let's have breakfast here. I'll make," he suggested.

We'd gone out to breakfast every morning. Now, when I need to go out more than ever, he wanted to "make"? "Sounds good," I lied. "Do you have eggs?"

"Yes."

Strike one. "Bacon?"

"Yes."

Strike two. "Potatoes?"

"Uh, no . . . but I can . . ."

*Oh, thank God.* "I'll go get some!" I jumped up, threw on some jeans, and headed out the door before he had the chance to stop me or tell me that he was allergic to potatoes. I ran full speed to the nearest store and made my way to the bathroom.

That afternoon we drove around a quiet part of the city. It was really pretty but I kept dozing off in the passenger seat. At one point he stopped and grabbed some fresh raspberries off a bush. I was starring in my own romantic comedy.

*"Framboises,"* he said as he handed them to me.

*"Merci,"* I said back. I was pretty sure that meant "raspberries are my favorite."

The drive to the airport that night was depressing, the flight home even more so. I got wrapped up in being his *geerlfrien* at the party, but once the moment passed I knew that I couldn't really be. What I wanted was somewhere in California and I had to go get it. There's a romantic me that has always wanted to be swept off her feet, but the realistic and ambitious me doesn't believe in the fantasy—and if a guy tries too hard I end up thinking he's a pussy. While I flew back to my dad's, I wondered if it was normal that I'd rather serve chili dogs to a bunch of overpaid frat guys than let a hot French Canadian guy steal my heart.

## TRUNDLE BEDS AND MASTURBATORS

A few months after I moved in with my dad, a girl I knew from Arkansas, Sarah Tilley, also moved to Los Angeles. She was living in Hollywood but didn't know many people. She wasn't someone I was really friends with. She was the ex-girlfriend of my friend Logan and I actually didn't like her. When they broke up he was heartbroken, so I thought she was a bitch. When he let me know that she was moving close to where I was, I asked him why I should care.

"Because you have hardly any friends there and sometimes when I talk to you you sound like you have a really bad cold, but I know that you are one of those freaks who rarely get sick," he responded.

"The air is different here. And I can't hang out with her since she hurt you."

"I'm over it, she and I get along fi—"

"What's her phone number? Does she have plans to-night?"

Yes, I had some friends at work but the pool was small and karaoke with my dad was getting old. I was way too excited for *General Hospital* every day. It was no longer tuning in for the paternity tests and the comas. I was tuning in to see familiar faces. I needed more of a life.

My addiction to *GH*—that's what the fans call it—was also costing me too much money. I had developed an affinity for something called "Soap Talk." It's a phone line that reels you in by telling you that you can call, choose option 5, and get some good spoilers. Then you learn that if you press 9 you can leave a message with your own thoughts on the lat-est storylines. You can be heard. I used to lie in bed at night and think maybe, just maybe, if I leave a convincing enough message they will hear my rational voice and finally let Sonny and Brenda get back together for good. I would drunkenly call the 900 number and leave messages for some poor in-tern who had to filter through voice mails from seventy-five-year-old divorcées and me. The first time Shirley confronted me with my $450 phone bill my legs went numb. She was worried I was calling some sort of sex chat line. She didn't seem relieved when I explained to her I was simply calling a daytime soap opera hotline. It probably would have been easier to learn that her new stepdaughter was a sex addict as opposed to a loser. I needed to get out more.

Sarah Tilley and I got in touch and planned to meet at a bar. I was kind of nervous. I started worrying about what it would be like if I still didn't like her—or, even worse, she didn't like me. I said a quick prayer that she and I would get along, certain that God had time in his busy schedule to make sure that I landed a drinking buddy.

Within minutes of polishing off our first drink, Sarah and I became friends. We both admitted we were nervous about hanging out, then both clarified that we were not lesbians, and went on with the night.

We met a handful of guys at the bar that night and introduced ourselves by last name in order to avoid confusion. I was really impressed with Tilley's ability to get guys' attention. She seemed to have no inhibitions about approaching them, which was really good for me. My hair still hadn't grown out.

One of the nights that she and I were out, we met this guy that she liked and he wanted to take us to an "after-hours" bar. I didn't know what that meant, but I liked the sound of it.

In my head it would be the kind of party I used to go to in college. I assumed that it stayed open later than it was supposed to and discreetly served alcohol in big red cups. It wasn't. It was a weird house on a dark street and in order to get in we needed a code word. The guy we followed there shouted "Banana cream pie!" into the speaker at the door and we were quickly buzzed into the secret club. Immediately I regretted agreeing to go to that party. There was a little bar set up and the house was barely lit. There were folding chairs, tiny tables, and a filthy couch. Someone offered me a seat on it, but I opted to stand since I was fairly certain sitting on it would get me pregnant. Tilley was a little less freaked out than I was, but she was still on high alert. A woman walked by with a small tray and stopped in front of us.

"Line?" she asked.

"Oh, I'm sorry, we didn't realize. We just walked right in," I replied.

"No, do you want a line?" She nodded toward her tray.

I looked down at what she was carrying and saw that on her cute little tray were big fat lines of blow. I'd never seen cocaine in person, but I was pretty sure she wasn't offering us a baby powder sample. She pulled two small straws out of her cleavage and offered them to us.

"I'm good. I don't want to end up Regina'd," I told her.

She looked at me like I was dumb, then to Tilley, who shook her head and waved the girl off.

"Oh my God, I'm so glad you're not a cokehead," I sighed in relief.

"What the hell does 'Regina'd' mean?" she asked.

Hadn't anybody else read *Sweet Valley High*? "Never mind, but can we get out of here? I'm really uncomfortable and I think I just felt a cockroach go up my pants."

Tilley agreed to getting out of there and we made our way toward the exit. When we got to the street we heard someone yelling after us. It was the guy we had followed there. I'd forgotten about him.

"Hey! Wait up! Where are you guys going?" he asked.

"Um, not really our scene. We kind of want to go dancing," Tilley responded. Even though I hated dance clubs, I nodded in agreement with her.

"Oh, I know a sweet place to dance. Also—look, I have this . . ." He reached into his pocket and I stepped back, ready for him to pull out a gun or perhaps some heroin. Instead he waved a yellow flyer in our faces.

"Two for one. I can get two of us in for the price of one cover charge. You girls have cash? I don't have any on me."

"You have a *coupon*?" Tilley asked, disgusted. "You have a coupon and you don't even have the cash to cover *your half* of the *coupon*?" I burst out laughing. My Southern accent was already fading, but hers was going strong, which made her coupon statement that much better.

The guy stared blankly at us. We left.

Just when I was at the end of my rope—I was still living with my dad and driving an hour back and forth to Los Angeles to take a crappy acting class—Tilley called me to see if I wanted to move in with her. She had a one-bedroom that she'd been sharing with a girl who was moving back to Arkansas. I wished it was a two-bedroom but I evaluated my living situation and determined that I didn't have a ton of room to be picky. I quickly announced to Dad and Shirley that I was moving up to Los Angeles. They pretended to be sad but I could see them immediately calculating what they'd be saving on booze and the phone bill alone.

Since we only had the one bedroom, my dad gave Tilley and me a trundle bed, which is basically a fucked-up bunk bed. One bed fits right under the other to save space, then at night when you pull it out, *voilà*—you have two beds. It's pretty embarrassing for anyone over the age of six to be sleeping on, but I didn't care. I was so happy to be finally living in L.A. and to start building a real life for myself. Outside of noticing right away that Tilley liked to open drawers and closets and not close them, living with her felt manageable.

There was a bar right down the street called Bird's. They served strong drinks and chicken and it was within walking distance of our new place, although I preferred to take a cab.

One night we'd been out late at Bird's and both fell

asleep in the living room. I woke up to the sound of Tilley gasping. I assumed she was just developing lung cancer since at the time we both smoked like we were getting paid for it. I saw her headed for the front door in a panic and I realized something bad was happening. I mean if she had lung cancer it would have been bad, but this seemed like it was bad for *me*.

I saw a guy coming through the door. When she went toward him, he backed out and she slammed the door shut. She screamed for me to call 911. I quickly dialed emergency and explained to the operator that a man had attempted to enter our apartment.

"Did he break in?" the operator inquired.

"I guess. We were asleep, so we definitely didn't invite him."

"Where is the man now?"

"Where is he now?" I asked Tilley.

She looked out the window, then jumped back about four feet.

"He's across the street!" she cried.

"He's across the street!" I yelled into the phone.

"Okay, stay calm. Can you see what he's doing?"

"Well, what's he doing?" I asked Tilley. "This woman is grilling me."

"He's just kind of standing there, staring," she answered.

"Does he have a weapon?" I threw that question out there myself. I was doing a better job than the 911 operator.

"Wait. Oh my God, he's jacking off!" Tilley shrilled.

"Oh my God, he's jacking off!" I cried into the phone.

"The police are on their way."

While we waited for the cops to show up, I decided to keep an eye out for the masturbator. I cracked open the door, chain lock solidly in place. I spotted him and made eye contact with him.

"What are you doing?" I asked.

"Sorry, I was just jacking off."

After that incident I had trouble getting a good night's sleep. Tilley started staying at her boyfriend's house more often, which was great for her but shitty for me. I spent several nights lying wide awake wondering if that would have happened to me in Arkansas. I didn't want to think about it. If I allowed myself to get nostalgic for "back home" every time something questionable happened in California, I wouldn't have lasted long. I also decided not to tell any of my parents about the masturbator. I didn't want them to worry.

I went on the hunt for a job in L.A. After looking for a couple of weeks, I got hired at a place named Smokin' Johnnie's and right under the sign it read BOOZE, BLUES, AND BBQS! It was a shithole just over the hill on Ventura Boulevard in Studio City. It had a dirty bathroom, plastic tables, and a sticky floor. The clientele was exactly what you'd expect from that description. But the ribs were pretty amazing.

I was not thrilled with coming home every night smelling like pulled pork, but I was happy to have a job. I was making money; I just needed to stay positive. I certainly wasn't going to get discovered by an agent or meet any guys at this crappy place, but at least I could afford to keep my side of the trundle bed warm. One afternoon—because I still didn't get scheduled for the night shifts—I worked a big party of about thirty people. The manager, who was pretty repulsive, was foaming at the mouth at the amount of money these people were spending. It wasn't a lot, but since the average lunch table spent seventeen dollars—for two—he was pumped. Nothing there was organized, the cooks were laughably slow, and the layout was stupid, so I ran around like an asshole all day. I constantly refilled iced teas and picked up wads and wads of dirty, BBQ-stained napkins. *These people are animals,* I thought.

I was so happy when they left and my shift ended. The only thing that got me through that day was knowing I had made some pretty good money for once. With the "automatic gratuity on parties of six or more" rule, this might be my best shift ever. I walked over to my manager to get my payout. He slapped a twenty in my hand and winked at me.

"Good work, kiddo!" he beamed.

I looked down at the twenty dollars. "Oh, thanks!" I said. I thought it was nice he was giving me a little extra for my hard work. "Can I get the tip from the party? I want to go home."

"You have it right there!" He smiled.

I stared at him, confused. "But that's twenty dollars. Their bill was at least four hundred. We added fifteen percent gratuity. That's sixty dollars." I wondered if he was impressed with my quick math.

"We split it up. I booked the party and I helped you. That's your cut."

"My cut? It's my table. You're a *manager.* You aren't supposed to get a tip. And splitting it would be thirty dollars."

"Slow down . . . I booked the party . . ." He started to defend himself.

"You answered a fucking phone call, which is what a manager does. You didn't *book* anything. Give me the rest of my money. It isn't yours."

"This is how it works here," he said flatly and walked away.

There wasn't really anything I could do so I walked over to the reservation book and looked over my shift the next day. I was the only waitress scheduled and there was a party of twenty and another party of fifteen coming in. *I don't know why it's busy tomorrow, but I like it,* I thought. I flipped to the back of the book where all of the other waitresses' phone numbers were and ripped out the page. I figured this was fair; at least the next day he'd earn the tip he'd stolen from me today. He wasn't smart enough to have a backup contact list, but I was smart enough to make sure he'd be screwed.

My legs shook as I drove, crying, back to the apartment. I couldn't believe I'd just quit a job. I had no money saved and there was no way I was going to ask my parents for any. I've always had this *Don't worry, I'm fine* attitude, regardless of whether I'm actually fine. I don't want to depend on someone else. I think it comes from watching my mother struggle to regain her own identity once she and my father were divorced. Somewhere along the line she had to find her footing again. If I never lost my footing, I'd never have to find it.

I got home and started to feel panicked so I went over to the bar where Tilley worked to tell her about my day. When I filled her in, she grabbed her crazy Greek boss and told me to tell him the story.

"That's disgusting!" he yelled when I told him about the manager that had stolen my tips. "Don't worry, we have a job for you here. You start tomorrow."

"What?" I said, shocked.

"What?" Tilley asked.

"Yeah baby, don't worry," he said in his Greek accent. "Tomorrow. See you then."

He walked away.

"You didn't tell me you guys were hiring!" I said excitedly to Tilley.

"We aren't."

"Really? Then what's he talking about?"

We both looked over and noticed George yelling at one of the other waitresses. She argued with him for a second, then threw down her apron and left.

"I guess that's what he was talking about."

I wasn't special. It turns out that girl had been pissing George off daily and my sob story was all he needed to push him over the edge. I felt guilty for about half an hour, then remembered that I had ten dollars in my checking account.

Mirabelle turned out to be a great place to work. Aside from Tilley, I worked with a guy named Chris Franjola, who also did stand-up. That was one of the things that I wanted to do and I now had someone to talk about it with. We're friends to this day, and I even get to work with him.

After work we always went to the bar next door, called Red Rock. On any given night it was like a frat house, so I liked it. Mirabelle closed earlier than they did so we always headed over there for last call, then the bartender would let us stay and drink while he closed up. I made a habit of stopping by there after my Sunday brunch shifts with my co-worker Jackie. We'd always plan to have a Bloody Mary and go home but would end up sitting on the same stool in our black pants and white shirts until at least 1 A.M.

There was a manager named Barry who worked there and was always flirting with me. His face was acceptable, but he had a weird body. His waist was where his knees should be, so we called him "Lo-Waisted" behind his back. As I type this I realize that it probably isn't that funny to read, but it made us laugh.

I was never even the slightest bit attracted to Lo-Waisted, so one night I went home with him. I had been at the bar for at least six hours with no break from drinking other than to pee. Lo-Waisted offered to drive my car to his house, which, looking back, was no help. If he had truly wanted to assist me he would have driven my car to my house and then cabbed home; at least that's what he would have done if he weren't trying to get laid. I covered one eye so that I could see Jackie clearly and told her that Barry was going to give me a lift to his place.

"You're going home with Lo-Waisted because you're wasted," she laughed.

"Right?!" I giggled.

I said bye to her and the next thing I knew I was at Lo-Waisted's apartment. The only thing I remember from the drive was that I was glad I was not driving. His place was small but it didn't really matter since we went straight to the bedroom. We had uneventful sex, but I don't put all the blame on him since for most of it I was in a blackout. The next thing I knew, it was morning. I rolled over to see that I was lying in bed next to Lo-Waisted. *I need to start going home after my Sunday shifts,* I thought to myself.

He was dead asleep so I felt confident I could get out of there without waking him. I grabbed my clothes—my waitressing clothes—and put them back on. There isn't a worse feeling than that. I grabbed my black Reeboks and my shirt that said "Don Julio Rules," picked up my purse, and headed out the door. I was in a rush, but caught out of the corner of my eye that his apartment was disgusting. It had a funky smell and there was a piece of pizza sitting on the coffee table, all by itself. I officially hated Lo-Waisted.

When I got to the parking garage I couldn't remember where he had left my car. After a few minutes I finally spotted it, and I ran. Suddenly I was in a panic to leave. I didn't want him to wake up and come down to find me. I was barefoot, hopefully not pregnant, and really hungover. I just wanted to get home. I couldn't figure out how he had gotten my car into the spot it was in. I couldn't even open the door all the way; I had to turn my body into a pretzel and slide through. I felt like I couldn't get out of there fast enough. I threw the car in reverse and instantly heard a loud "crunch" sound. I looked behind me . . . thank God . . . not a person. Then I looked to my left and saw that I had hit a huge beam. In order to keep from doing worse damage, I'd need to go forward, do a bunch of quarter turns, and maneuver out. So I gunned it and let the beam scrape all the way down the side of my Mustang. I just wanted to get the fuck out of there. That car sucked anyway.

I didn't want to have to give up going to Red Rock, so the next day I went in with Jackie. When I saw Lo-Waisted, I just pretended that nothing had happened. I hugged him around his waist, which required me to bend my knees, then plopped down on a stool and ordered a vodka cranberry with an extra shot of vodka. He was too confused to do anything but follow my lead and act normal. Jackie was shocked.

"Really? That works?" she asked.

"Every time," I told her. "Guys are more insecure than we are. All you have to do is act like everything is fine.

They're just so relieved they don't have to deal with your feelings; they don't want to talk about it, either."

"But what if they like you? Lo-Waisted doesn't necessarily realize that you knowingly did permanent damage to your car just so you could get out of his garage."

"I know. That's why this works. Now he will be way too insecure to ask me out. He'll just chalk it up to a one-night stand and move on."

"Okay, so what if *you* like *them*?" she challenged me.

"I haven't figured that one out yet," I said, then polished off a plate of chicken fingers.

## HELL CAT

After several months of living in Los Angeles, I started to realize that I wasn't doing much to get my career going. I hadn't moved to L.A. to waitress, but the only productive thing I'd done outside of that was take a bad acting class. That wasn't going anywhere, since most of the time all the teacher had us do was sit in a chair in the middle of the room and conjure up emotions, which is what I already did at home.

Some of the waiters I worked with told me that I should take an improv class. They said it would come in handy for thinking on my feet during auditions. I nodded my head in agreement even though I had never been on an actual audition.

I flipped through the free weekly paper and found a cheap improv class in Sherman Oaks. I was nervous the first night, but it was just introductory. We all went around and said a little bit about ourselves in an attempt to get to know one another. There were a couple of people who stood out to me as someone I'd want to hang out with: a guy named Neil and a girl named Chelsea.

Chelsea seemed like fun and she quickly confirmed that she was. We had similar sensibilities and a similar affection for cocktails. Neil, on the other hand, was the exact opposite. He didn't drink at all. In fact, he told me he had never had a drink in his life.

"Never even a sip?" I challenged him.

"Never even a sip," he responded. "Why doesn't anyone ever believe me?"

"Because it just sounds so . . . so . . . dumb," I said.

"I guess that's what people think. But alcohol just doesn't interest me."

"Do you have a hard time getting along with people who drink?" He was cute, so I needed to know the answer to that question right away.

"Not at all. But usually people who like to drink have a hard time accepting that I don't."

"Well, that sounds really immature. How sad for them." Inside, I feared I might agree with "them."

But I figured his not drinking shouldn't be a big deal to me if my excessive drinking wasn't going to be a big deal to him. He also drove any time that we went out, which was kind of awesome.

Neil was new to town, via Florida. He told me that he had once performed for a week in Australia, so I felt like he had already made it in show business. Chelsea had also recently moved to L.A., so it felt good to have new friends who were trying to figure it out like I was.

The class itself was really stupid. Although I very much appreciate and respect people who are good at improv, I dislike doing it. That's probably because I suck at it. I can think on my feet; I just find the "games" annoying. Maybe that's why I always knew what I wanted to do. In acting, things are written for you. In stand-up, you write it yourself. In both, you don't have to ask the audience to help you come up with an uncomfortable scenario.

I introduced Chelsea to Red Rock and it was love at first drink. She enjoyed the clientele and the chicken wings. The latter part I was not thrilled about. I fucking hate watching people eat chicken wings, and Chelsea Handler is no exception. She sticks the whole thing in her mouth and ten seconds later pulls out a bare bone. It's like she's committing a crime and wiping the carcass clean of evidence. It's not just her; that's how everybody eats chicken wings. It's really gross and I don't get it. Why couldn't it be like eating a rib, where people nibble on it daintily until the meat is gone. I considered Chelsea lucky I didn't write her off based on how she ate.

My friendship with Neil was different from anything I could remember. He really intrigued me. For a while I thought he was gay, because I didn't know other guys who were that well dressed, funny, and into doing characters. I really wanted Neil to be impressed with me the way that I was with him. He'd traveled and was witty and he believed without a doubt that he was going to be successful. If he thought the same about me, maybe it would make it true.

I confirmed for myself that he was not gay one night after he spilled his guts about his ex-girlfriend in Florida that he was sad he'd left behind. It was obvious that he still cared for her, but he insisted that they were through.

"We still talk," he admitted. "But we're just friends."

"Being friends after you break up with someone is dumb," I lectured.

It was clear Neil was not emotionally available to fall in love with someone, so I developed a huge crush on him. Since I drank but he didn't, I acted like I drank less than I actually did. The responsible girl in me didn't want to chase him off until she knew for sure where the relationship was going. Luckily I've grown more comfortable with who I am, so now, if I meet a guy who tells me he doesn't drink, I tell him that things between us aren't going to work out.

Neil and I started hanging out constantly. If I wasn't at Red Rock with Chelsea, I was with Neil. His disinterest in alcohol meant that we did things like go to the movies or wander through art museums, but no matter what we did we had fun. We checked out bands and went for hikes. I saw a lot more of Los Angeles in the months after I met him than I had in the year prior. I thought it was kind of weird how much time I was spending with Neil. It made sense for him; he'd just moved to California and the only person he really knew was the guy he was staying with, Mark. They were acquaintances, which is why Mark had set up an air mattress for him in his spare room, but I had *friends*. I had Chris, I had Tilley. I had Jackie and my other friend Casey. I even had a couple who had moved out from Arkansas: Brandon and Liz. I felt pretty lucky in the support department. Regardless, for a while I made nearly all of my plans with Neil.

After three solid months of spending almost every day and night with me, Neil took a trip back to Florida to retrieve his two cats from his ex-girlfriend.

"That's so *great* that you are going to see her," I lied. "It's almost summer. I bet she's really tan!"

I know it sounds like I played it cool, but inside I was in turmoil over whether the two of them were going to fall back in love the second they laid eyes on each other. I wasn't sure if I was even allowed to have feelings about it, so I said that I didn't. We weren't officially boyfriend and girlfriend. We hadn't had sex. We'd spent almost every night together for the past few weeks, but we never did more than make out. I wasn't sure that asking him to be faithful to me was within my rights.

The night before Neil left for Florida, I stayed the night on his air mattress with him. I had a perfectly comfortable trundle bed at home, but I wanted to be where he was. That night I was sure that our kissing would lead to more, but it didn't. He looked at sex differently than I did; he thought that it meant something. I was pretty sure we weren't right for each other but every time I thought that he and I had zero in common, he'd make me laugh and our differences wouldn't seem important anymore. I started to think that maybe it was good we were different. Maybe that's what I needed. It was like Paula Abdul and that animated cat said: "Opposites attract."

Neil returned from his trip to Florida with a convertible and two cats.

"You aren't doing anything to squash people's thoughts that you're gay," I told him. "Why don't you just design a car shaped like a penis and drive that around town?"

He didn't care. He just laughed and said, "I lived in

Florida. Now I live in California. Not having a convertible
is a waste!" I envied his ability to not give a shit what people
thought.

I casually grilled Neil about his visit with his ex.

"HOW WAS IT!?" I screamed. "It must have been
GREAT to see her!?! So, was she PRETTY as ever?"

"It was okay," he replied.

"*Okay* as in you LOVE HER?" I subtly asked.

Neil laughed. "*Okay* as in we broke up months ago and
now we live in different states and I'm hanging out with
you." He smiled.

I smiled, too. "Hanging out" was good enough for me,
even though I wasn't positive what it meant.

Neil asked me if I could take his cats for a while.

"My roommate Mark isn't a cat guy. I need to leave
them with you until I find my own place."

"Uh, how long would I have them for?" I asked. I liked
cats but this seemed like a big job. I considered telling him
what Shirley told me when I asked her if I could bring my
cat with me when I moved in with her and Dad, which was
"I'm allergic," which is code for "I fucking hate cats."

"Just until I find my own place. I'm only living with
Mark until that happens."

"Okay, no problem." I actually liked cats, and I figured
that Tilley did as well. Most single girls do. So I took the
little fuckers, Mischief and Malki, and let them join us in
our sad one-bedroom, which was now starting to get a little
crowded.

If you've ever owned a cat, you know that they don't do
well with change. Any time that you move a cat from one
home to another, you need to keep them indoors for a couple of weeks so that they can get used to their surroundings;

otherwise they'll make a run for it. I don't know if they are trying to find their old home or just get the hell out of their new one, but either way they are not pleased being uprooted.

Both of the cats got out of the apartment within hours of being under my care. The area we were living in was known for having many coyotes, so the situation wasn't good. I didn't know how they escaped, but if faced with having to tell Neil, I planned to blame Tilley. Luckily she was also worried that they'd disappeared and joined me on a neighborhood hunt for Mischief and Malki. It was early afternoon and Neil was coming over that night to "visit" them, as if we were a divorced couple and these were our children. I needed to find them before he got there. He wasn't going to be in the mood to finally have sex with me if he found out I'd lost his cats.

Cats don't respond to being called by their name. They don't even really respond to being called. They just do what they want to do on their time and if you would like to get them to do something for you, well good fucking luck. The worst part was that I didn't even really know what they looked like. I knew that they were black. That was it. Tilley and I drove around the neighborhood and if we saw a black cat we'd yell "Mischief? Malki?" out the window. No response didn't mean it was or wasn't one of them. It just meant we'd seen a black cat. It was sort of racist.

After a few grueling hours of searching, we returned to our apartment. I had decided that I would just have to come clean with Neil about the cats being gone. That is—I was still going to blame Tilley.

Defeated, we pulled into our parking spot. Tilley told me she was sure that Neil would understand, although she agreed that this was not going to help the sex situation. When we got to our front door, both of the cats were there. They were staring at us expectantly, with a look that said, "Open the door, assholes."

I couldn't believe those little shits had come back! How did they even know where the apartment was? I quickly decided that cats were geniuses and I made a mental note to donate lots of money to cat organizations as soon as I had some extra cash. I needed to reward them for coming back. We didn't have many groceries, but once we got inside I popped open a can of ravioli and let the two of them go nuts. Neil was coming over in an hour and he'd never need to know that for a few hours I had misplaced his beloved pets.

I felt like the return of his cats had earned me some sex, but since I didn't want to tell him the story, I couldn't use it for seduction. Instead I simply enjoyed a movie and some shitty Chinese food with Neil. I found myself sleeping peacefully next to him that night. I realized I must really be falling for him, since not doing it actually felt like the right thing to do.

A few weeks later, our improv class was about to have its first big show. We rehearsed weekly and other classes acted as our audience, as we'd do for them, but this was going to be the first time we had a real *paying* audience. I invited my dad and Shirley, along with a few other friends.

I was nervous about the show, but Neil calmed me down. Something about him made me feel really secure and the night went off without a hitch. The audience had a great time and my dad thought I was hilarious. I was sure it had *nothing* to do with us being related.

The next day I decided to reward myself. I went to Melrose Avenue to go shopping. I also had a date with Neil that night, so I figured I might as well look really cute. A good outfit could only help my chances for premarital sex.

When you move to L.A., people tell you that Melrose is the place to shop but they are lying. Maybe they aren't intentionally lying; maybe they are just misled. Either way, shopping on Melrose is dumb, and it was even dumber in 1998. It seems like it's cost-friendly and you're getting a good deal, but really it's cheap, shitty clothing made to look decent by stores that play cool music and have hip-looking people working in them. I tried on a million outfits before I decided on a pair of brown and green plaid pants that way over-accentuated my already meaty thighs and a tank top that felt like it was sewn together by the blind. Those stores hire the right people, though. I walked out of there feeling confident that I had spent that ninety-five dollars well.

That night, Neil, his friend Ryan, and I went to the Hollywood Improv to see Chelsea perform her first semiprofessional stand-up set. It was a blast and everybody was gracious enough to not mention that it looked like my pants were splitting above the knee.

Chelsea wanted to go out after her show and I wanted to go with her. She had such a great set, it felt like we needed to celebrate. Neil wanted to go home. I found myself, as I often do to this day, not sure how to please a boyfriend and a girlfriend at the same time. I looked at Neil for help with my decision.

"You should go with her," he said.

"Really?" I was confused. "That's so sweet. Are you sure?" *Why is this so easy? Shouldn't he want me to go home with him? Usually guys are jerks about this. Wait, did he just break up with me?*

"This is a big deal, and she's one of your best friends. I just don't feel like going out. I'll go home with Ryan."

I kissed Neil on the cheek. "You're pretty great," I told him. Then I hopped in the car with Chelsea.

We had so much fun that night. We toasted her success and more to come. Between her and Neil, I felt like I was really getting involved in the world of comedy. I was so glad I had these two people in my life.

The next day I went to Palm Springs with my dad. He had some friends there and they had invited us down for the day to swim and lie around by their pool. Those were two of my favorite things to do, so I was excited. I reminded Dad over and over that I had to be back early evening, though. We had improv rehearsal and Neil and I had planned to go together.

I kept trying to call Neil all day to figure out what time to be ready, and to find out if we were doing something after so I'd know what bad outfit from Melrose to wear. I also wasn't enjoying Palm Springs, which made no sense since I'd been so looking forward to the trip. I just wanted to get back to L.A. It didn't help that my many attempts at reaching Neil went unanswered. I figured that even though he said he was fine with it, he must have been mad at me for going out. It was driving me crazy that he wouldn't return my call.

Later that night, after still no response from Neil, I got a call from his roommate, Mark. Mark wanted to let me know that Neil wasn't mad at me.

"I know you've called him a bunch of times. I just wanted to get back to you," Mark said.

"Oh, thanks," I said, confused. "Sorry if his phone was going off a ton. Did he forget to take it with him?"

I tried to sound upbeat but I knew it wasn't good that Mark was the one calling me. It kind of felt like when I used to call people on three-way when I was in high school in order to bust one person saying bad shit about the other, but it didn't seem like Neil was secretly on the other line.

"Neil was in an accident," Mark told me. "I'm sorry I didn't call you back earlier, but I've had to call a lot of people," he said.

"Oh my God!" I said. "This is awful. Tell me what hospital he's in. I'll go right there. I feel so dumb, I've thought all day that he was mad at me, when he's just laid up in a hospi—"

"He didn't make it," he replied. "He's dead."

I just sat there. All day there'd been that unexplainable feeling in the pit of my stomach. I'm not claiming that I have some sort of ESP, but I do think sometimes when bad things happen to people we love, we know before we really know.

"Is Ryan . . . how is Ryan?"

"He's dead, too. They were driving the convertible. A drunk driver hit them on Laurel Canyon. I'm sorry, but I have to go. His family has been calling all day. I don't know how to handle it."

Mark hung up.

Laurel Canyon Boulevard is one of those narrow, curvy roads. He and Ryan had no chance when the other guy crossed the centerline. Now a man who had never had a drink in his life had been killed by a drunk driver. And I had told him to go home without me.

I didn't know Neil for years, so I don't want to make his death about me. He had a mother and he had family and he had friends who had loved him for a long time. I am so glad I got to know him for the short time that I did.

My mom told me that if something would have happened to me right after I moved away from home she would have been even more sad to think I felt alone. So I wrote his mom a letter to let her know that that wasn't the case for Neil. That he had friends.

A couple weeks after sending the letter, I got one back. It wasn't from his mom, though—it was from Jenny, his ex-girlfriend. The only difference between Jenny and what Neil told me about Jenny was that when she wrote me the letter, she referred to herself as Neil's girlfriend. She said that they were together up until the night that he had died, and that he had told her a lot about his "friend Sarah."

He had never broken up with her. *Maybe that was why we never had sex,* I thought. All this time I assumed it was his conservative ways scaring him off when in fact he had a girlfriend. I tried to look at the bright side: At least he didn't cheat on her. He lied, but he didn't cheat—well, he didn't fully cheat. I assume that was his logic, anyway.

In her letter, Jenny offered to take the cats back. By that point Malki had already gotten back out into the canyon, but this time he did not return. I assume he went via coyote. I decided to keep Mischief, mostly because it seemed like trying to get a cat to Florida would be a pain in the ass. He wasn't very old, so I had to have him neutered, which drained my bank account. I cursed Neil and his lies as I signed the vet bill. That fucking cat still lives with me to this day and he doesn't appear to be aging.

Sometimes he looks at me funny when I'm naked.

# THE LIST

**S**everal months after Neil died, I was still working at Mirabelle when one of the regulars offered me a day job at a commercial production company. I was just going to be a receptionist, but he made it sound fancy by talking about how I would learn so much and that maybe one day they could even cast me in one of their ads. He didn't bother to mention to me that it was a Hispanic commercial company and that the fact I was white would probably keep me out of the running. He wanted in my pants, but at the time I didn't realize it. I've had lots of male friends throughout my life. I've never been one to assume that just because a guy wants to be close to me he wants to be inside of me. Sometimes that keeps me from being disappointed, and sometimes it gets me felt up in commercial production offices.

My new boss was named Mel. He was short with red hair and had several obvious insecurities. I thought it was funny to call him "Mellybean," but he put the hammer down on that quickly. Apparently when he was little, kids would call him "Smelly Melly," which scarred him for life. I personally thought it was hilarious, and I wish I had a friend named Mel now so that I could use that. Plus he needed to learn to take a joke; I was called "Colonna Bologna" all through middle school, and I turned out great.

I found myself behind a desk trying to type up invoices and send out FedEx packages five days a week. I had no idea what I was doing. Smelly Melly didn't seem to care, though. He was too busy trying to put his hand up my shirt.

Smelly Melly was married. His wife was a beautiful, busty blonde. The two of them together made absolutely no sense. I couldn't figure out what she saw in him, until one day I came across his tax return in the file cabinet. I was shocked to find out what kind of money people earned by simply making commercials, especially ones that aired on Telemundo. I felt sort of guilty for finding out what his income was, but at the same time I was relieved to know that his wife was a gold digger rather than a kidnap victim, which is what I had assumed. My fantasy went something like this: She was vacationing in Cancún and he was there filming a commercial for Jose Cuervo. He spotted her on the beach, but she walked right past him since he is two feet shorter and much less attractive than her. She simply hadn't noticed him, but he thought he was being snubbed. Suddenly all he could hear was the kids from his school chanting "Smelly Melly! Smelly Melly! You'll never find a wife that has a small belly!" He snapped. He followed her to her hotel and slipped in behind her when she went into her room. He put a rag over her mouth and she passed out. When she woke up she was married to an angry redhead who had scared her into believing that if she tried to get away he'd kill her entire family. That was the only way he'd have been able to marry such a hot woman. That was before I knew that he was a millionaire.

It quickly became obvious that Smelly Melly and the blonde did not have a stable relationship. I often heard him on the phone yelling at his wife while I sat in my office and prayed that he would fire me. He acted like I couldn't hear a thing. Instead of making me contact therapists for the anger issues I am assuming he had, he grabbed me by my hips and sat me in his lap like he was a mall Santa. I'd get up and tell him to leave me alone, and he'd laugh it off like he was joking around and I was taking it way too seriously.

Nobody in the office was a decent person. One of the partners was a pudgy Hispanic man with a beard and a bad attitude. He was really picky about his lunch, even though it was always from Subway. One day he ordered his usual ham sandwich and asked me to make certain it was "Virginia ham." I rolled my eyes and went to get him the same ham sandwich I'd gotten him every day for the past three months. When I returned I was in mid-thought about whether or not picking up lunch was actually the job of the receptionist when Angry Hispanic Partner Guy snatched the sandwich out of my hand.

"Is this Virginia ham?" he asked curtly.

"It's ham," I replied. "They only have one kind."

"I only eat Virginia ham!" he exploded. "Did you make sure that's what you ordered?"

"It's the same thing you've been eating since I started working here."

"Go back and make sure it's Virginia ham."

"It's Subway. You're lucky if it's from a pig, let alone Virginia," I told him. "This job is stupid and your partner is a pervert. Get your lunch yourself, and maybe try choking on it," I said calmly. Then I left and never returned. Fuck that noise.

I was making enough money waiting tables that I felt like I didn't need to have my ass grabbed by a sex-crazed redhead's hand every morning at 8 A.M. or try to locate what fucking farm a piece of ham was raised on. So far the only perk of the job had been the one time Christopher McDonald came into the office. He was my favorite from *Thelma & Louise,* and when he walked into the building I got butterflies. It was the only moment that I thought I might actually be working at a legitimate company. It turned out he was at the wrong address. I pointed him in the right direction and fantasized that I worked at the office that he had been looking for in the first place. It was probably a real production company where they had several selections of ham and none of them was from Subway.

I did meet a cute guy while I was working there. He worked in production of some sort and drove an old VW bus. He was tall and scruffy, just how I like them. I've probably only gone out with two guys who fit that description in my life, and neither of them lasted for more than a few weeks. My "type" never makes for a great boyfriend, but they're usually pretty good in bed.

His name was Ben and he was kind of a mess, but he was really cute. He had a lack of responsibility that I found endearing. At times it's fun to date a guy who doesn't seem to care about anything, like the times I'm feeling lost and want to seem as if I have my shit together.

The first time we went out, Ben took me to an Italian place in Venice Beach. Taking me to a family-owned Italian restaurant always scores huge points. Someone once tried to take me to an Olive Garden, so I made him take me home.

The restaurant was great. Romantic atmosphere, great food, good wine. The only bummer was that he picked me up, so I had to ride in his old VW bus for forty minutes. The windows rattled, and if we went over a small bump it felt like the whole car would collapse. I can't stand people who think it's cool to drive old fucked-up cars that barely function, just because they're vintage. It seems like an excuse not to buy a new car, and it usually is.

He paid for dinner, so at least he had some manners. I'd been out with enough "let's go dutch" guys since I'd moved to L.A., and I had zero interest in going out with another. I don't give a shit what people say about feminism, equality, whatever; every girl wants the guy to get the check on the first date. If they say they don't mind, they're lying.

After seeing the inside of his van I certainly didn't want to see his apartment. If it was even a quarter as dirty, I'd never be able to lie on any of his furniture, and what I had in mind for that night required me to be on my back. I knew Tilley wouldn't be home, so we went back to my place.

I decided I wanted to be sexy so I made him wait on the couch while I covered the bathroom with white candles, undressed, and called him in to join me in the bathtub—which I had filled with bubbles—so that we could have sex. The next day, when I told Tilley about my romantic night, she reminded me that only last week the bathtub had backed up and we'd spent hours scrubbing brown sludge out of it.

"That's nasty," she scolded me. "We have no idea what the hell was coming out of that drain."

"I forgot."

"Forgot? It took us three hours to clean out! Gross. The only time bathtub sex is hot is at a hotel or if you have one of those big fancy tubs. We have a crappy old rusty one and last week there was shit in it."

"Oh my God, I had sex in a bathtub that had shit in it."

"That's what I just said. Maybe call your gyno and go get a checkup. So do you like him? Are you going out again?"

"I don't think so," I told her. "He's pretty cute, but I don't think he works more than once a month. I want to date someone with a little more ambition."

"So you had sex with him because you knew it wasn't going anywhere?" she asked.

"Exactly!" I replied, excited that I had a friend in L.A. who really understood me.

Tilley and I eventually graduated to a two-bedroom apartment. It was in a very busy area, right behind a bar named Tom Bergen's. Bergen's is an old Irish pub and they have shamrocks all over the walls and ceiling with celebrities' names written on them boasting who has come in over the years. When I saw Kiefer Sutherland's shamrock I knew the bar was my kind of place.

I called the area we lived in the concrete jungle. That was before Jay-Z called New York a concrete jungle and made it sound cool. It was a shitty gray neighborhood and the only view was asphalt. We were on the second floor and the heat pounded right through our sad little balcony door. The only air-conditioning was a tiny window unit and you could only feel cool air if you stood right in front of it and positioned your head just a little to the right. It was so bad that I actually missed the trundle bed.

I had been doing stand-up pretty regularly since I had left the dumb production job, and I was still working at Mirabelle. Chelsea was still doing comedy, too, so we went around to places together and got to know a lot of comics. A few of the places we went were okay, but most of them sucked. She even dragged me to a Starbucks across from the Beverly Center mall one night.

"We're doing stand-up at Starbucks?"

"Yes," she told me. "I know it sounds dumb but it's supposed to be a good crowd."

We walked in and there were two people there. Neither was there for comedy; they were there for Frappuccinos. Apparently the woman who "booked" it also forgot to show up, so the angry girl working at the counter helped us plug in an amp in the corner and told us to "have fun."

Chelsea made me go first, and I quickly scared off the two people in the room.

"Next week I'll try to get us a gig at Jamba Juice," she told me as we walked out.

"You aren't even gonna buy a latte?" I heard the angry counter girl yell as the door shut behind us.

A few nights later we were out at yet another bad open mic and I met this guy named Kevin. Kevin was a redhead and a comic. The red hair bugged me; I still had a bad taste in my mouth from my experience with Smelly Melly. Kevin was cute, though. He was from Boston and had a fun accent. We'd just met and he was being really flirtatious with me. I liked how bold he was.

Turns out, he wasn't bold: He was just drunk. He got my email from a mutual friend and the next day wrote me a long email apologizing for hitting on me. I started to get kind of annoyed as I was reading it. Nobody wants to wake up to an email from a guy that says, "I'm so sorry I hit on you, I was drunk out of my mind." But he redeemed himself at the end of the email by saying that he thought I was cute and he wondered if I'd give him a chance to go out with him sober. I agreed, hoping the "sober" part was just him being funny.

On our first date, we hit it off pretty well. He wasn't the kind of guy who made me laugh out loud, but he made me smile with his jokes and on top of it he seemed really responsible. Comedy was more of just something he was trying, but he didn't expect it to pay his bills. He wore button-down shirts and had a job at Universal Studios. I never really understood what he did there, but it was a real job and he had health benefits. I was a little tired of dating losers, so his togetherness appealed to the part of me that was looking to get *my* shit together.

The night I had met Kevin he'd been in rare form. It turned out he wasn't a big drinker at all. He started work at 8 A.M. every weekday and was in bed by 10 P.M. every weeknight. Once in a while he'd have a little fun on the weekends, but that usually just meant he'd stay up until eleven. I wasn't sure how our lifestyles were going to fit together, but I was determined to give it a try. It was time for something to change.

Kevin and I became boyfriend and girlfriend, and I liked it. I had missed having a boyfriend. Tilley had one. Chris Franjola and her had started dating, and they were having fun. I didn't want to be the single friend anymore, and now I wasn't. Finally when Tilley would come home and tell me funny stories about her and Chris, I could relate. If he did something to piss her off, I knew what that was like because I had a boyfriend, too. If he made her laugh, chances were good that Kevin had almost made me laugh that day, so I could just punch up the story and make it seem like he was a blast.

In the meantime, Chelsea and I continued to go to Red Rock. I tried really hard to just stay home and watch TV with Kevin, but I found it very daunting. I was annoyed that though he seemed like such a good time the night that I'd met him, he was more of a wet blanket. For the most part he wanted to order in and rent a movie. I liked that sometimes, I really did—but I didn't like it five nights a week. I found myself pretending I'd get off work later than I actually did so that I could stay out past midnight without pissing him off.

I wasn't doing anything wrong when I was out. I never cheated on him. I just wasn't ready to spend every night on the couch. At the same time I wasn't ready to go back to being single. I was sure that I was supposed to be with someone like Kevin and that if I could just be myself when he wasn't around I could be the kind of girlfriend he wanted when he was.

Since I loved waking up with a boyfriend, I'd go to his apartment even if I was out past his bedtime. I had a key, which made me feel very adult, and if I was "working late" he told me to just let myself in. The next morning I'd stir a little while he got ready for his important job, then I'd fall right back to sleep for a couple of hours and go to my place later, after I ate breakfast, since he kept a well-stocked fridge. All I had in my apartment was a tub of whipped cream, which I was never able to look at the same again after the time I came home drunk and opened some, saw a huge handprint right down the middle, and noticed that Tilley's bedroom door was closed.

Kevin's irritation with my love of drinking was growing. He didn't think it was as cute as I did that I liked to stay at Red Rock until 3 A.M. Since so far the only really impressive thing he'd done was get some of my friends into Universal Studios for free, I wasn't sure why he acted like he was so much better than me or the people I hung out with. He thought it was time that I grew up, but I was only a couple of years into my twenties.

You'd think I would have just broken up with him, but that didn't really occur to me. I was still new to L.A. and I wanted someone to be in the trenches with. I didn't realize yet that it was enough to have good friends. I was searching for what everyone back home told me they already had.

One morning after Kevin went to work I decided to sit at his desk and do some writing. I wanted to feel productive, but if I went home to my place I would usually get distracted and end up at happy hour searching for shamrocks of old TV stars. I spotted a notebook and went to rip some paper out of it when I noticed my name at the top of a page. Underneath my name there was what looked like a list. I'm not one of those people who have the willpower to shut a notebook when it clearly says something about them. I still, at thirty-six, peek at my presents when I go home for Christmas. Patience isn't one of my strong suits.

The page with my name on it was full of dates and abbreviations. It read something along the lines of:

11/7 RR w/CH 2 am call
11/8 RR w/ST 1 am call

And the list went on. It took me little time to figure out that "RR" was Red Rock, "CH" was Chelsea Handler, and "ST" was Sarah Tilley. There were other names and bars, but you get the idea. Kevin was keeping a list of when I went out, who I went out with, and what time I called him to let him know that I was coming over. It was pretty fucking creepy.

I immediately called Chelsea to tell her what I had found. She suggested I gather my things, go home, and never speak to Kevin again. I agreed with the "never speak to him again" part, but I had to confront him first.

"What are you going to say to him?" she asked.

"Just that I found this, that it's borderline illegal, and that I'm breaking up with him."

"I'm glad to hear that you draw the line at what appears to be stalking."

"Thanks. If I'm not at Red Rock by eight tonight, have the police check his dumpster for my head."

I hung up and called Kevin.

He got really excited when he heard my voice. "Hey! What 'cha up to?" he said with his annoying Boston accent.

"Oh, I'm still at your place. I thought I'd sit down and write for a bit."

"Great! Come up with any new stuff?" he asked.

"I have a pretty good story, actually. It's not all fleshed out yet, but it should get a good laugh when I tell it onstage," I said drily. "Anyway, I borrowed some paper out of your notebook. Hope that's okay."

"Sure, why would I care if you borrowed paper?"

"Well, if you run out of paper how are you going to log my nightly activities?"

He was silent for a few seconds.

"Oh, that!" he laughed. "That's my notes for *my* stand-up!"

"You're writing jokes about what time I come home and

what bars I go to? Sorry to be the bearer of bad news, but those jokes aren't funny."

"No, it's just . . . you do so many funny little things . . . ha ha ha ha, I just thought I should write them down so I can talk about my girlfriend in my act, you know?" He was really reaching.

"These aren't 'funny little things' that I do. You didn't write down that I alphabetize my CDs or that I set my alarm three times in a row before going to bed; you wrote down where I go and who I'm with!"

We went back and forth for a little bit, but he finally admitted that he was keeping tabs on me. He said that he felt like I went out way too much for someone who was in a relationship and that he started to write it down so that when he approached me about it, he'd have ammunition. He was correct, I did go out too much, but keeping a journal of it wasn't any better.

"How about just saying 'I think you go out too much'?" I asked him. "That would have been far more efficient."

I told him that there was no way we were dating anymore and hung up. I grabbed my stuff, went to my car, checked underneath for a bomb, and drove home. I was a little relieved because I knew he wasn't the right guy for me in the long run, but I found myself crying and I wasn't sure why I felt sad at all.

The me now knows why it hurt. I was living far away from my family. I was a waitress, and I was broke. Having a boyfriend made me feel like I was doing one thing right, and now that that was over I was back to doing everything wrong.

When I got home I told Tilley what happened and she started laughing. I stared at her, wondering where the sympathy was, then a few seconds later I started laughing, too. I got myself ready and went to meet CH at RR. When it turned 1 A.M. I was relieved that I didn't have to call anybody to check in, and that in turn nobody could write down what time I had called.

# BIKINI ROCK BOTTOM

Shortly after I ended things with Kevin, I booked my first commercial. I was more excited than you can imagine. I finally had my first acting job and I had gotten it all on my own. I felt a new sense of independence.

The commercial was for Sprint Canada. I played a girl who sees Candice Bergen on a plane and tells her all about how I met a guy on vacation in Greece and we stayed in touch through Sprint Canada and now we're engaged. It reminded me of Marc. Yes, we met in Mexico, not Greece. We stayed in touch through email, not Sprint. We were not engaged; in fact we hadn't talked for a few months. Other than that, this commercial *was* our relationship.

My mom found it very disappointing that my first acting job wouldn't be airing in the United States, but I assured her there were many more to come and that this particular job was really just a sign for me to get back in touch with Marc. I figured since he lived in Canada, he'd probably see the commercial. The least he deserved was a heads-up. I was so excited for a reason to reach out to him since I was completely bored in the guy department. I emailed him and anxiously awaited a response, but after a couple of weeks with no word, I assumed I wasn't going to hear back.

I did realize that booking a commercial wasn't a career maker, especially when it only aired in Canada. I was a few months from turning twenty-five and so far my life wasn't turning out as planned. But at least I was more hopeful now.

I met another comic, Ira Goldstein, and thought he was really cute. He did stand-up and had a job doing promos at NBC. The latter part was nice because he had a real job, like Kevin had, but it sounded more fun and he seemed to like it. I'd gone for responsible, and I'd gone for complete messes; with Ira I sensed something different. He had that funny-but-responsible combo that I really needed. Funny would keep me from getting bored and responsible would keep me from getting unemployment.

I didn't care that Ira was Jewish. In fact, I didn't realize he was until Chris Franjola explained to me that the name "Ira Goldstein" might as well be "Jewey Jew-Jew." One thing about growing up in a small town in Arkansas was that I was really sheltered from anything but plain old white Southern people. This can go two ways: You can either emerge really closed-minded and slightly racist, or you can be so used to seeing everybody the same way that you continue to do that, no matter who you meet. I like to believe I emerged the latter. When I told my grandpa that I was dating a Jewish guy he asked, "So he's cheap?" He emerged the former.

I hadn't spent much time with Ira. We'd had a couple of good conversations in which we both figured out that we loved bad movies and Mötley Crüe. There was something very sweet about him, but also very smart. He was a lot different from the other guys I had dated, and as far as I was concerned, that was a good thing.

He called me one afternoon and asked me if I wanted to go to something called Burning Man. It's a big outdoor festival in the middle of a desert where people congregate and some display their creativity through art, music, or a really dumb costume. I think it used to actually mean something, but now it's just a place to go for a week to do mushrooms and ecstasy. Ira had told me that he was going with a few guys, and one had backed out. He offered me the fall-out spot.

I said yes without really thinking, which trumped Quebec as the most spontaneous thing I'd ever done. I still do very few things that aren't well thought out, with the exception of sex. I told myself that in agreeing to do this I was really branching out, then went to my friend's house and borrowed an eighties prom dress so that I could fit in for costume night.

Getting to the festival requires flying to Reno, then driving for a couple of hours. Ira and his friends had already rented an RV, which we'd be sleeping in. All I had to do was get on a plane, which was perfect because outside of that I didn't know what the fuck I was doing. I was nervous.

Once I landed in Reno and met up with Ira I felt better—he was way too adorable to have friends who would gang-rape me. In fact I started to realize that it was a bold move for him to invite a girl he didn't know that well to the desert with his two best friends for four days. I knew how brutal guys could be from my own male friends. I focused on not seeming drunk and stumbled over to introduce myself to his buddies. After a slight delay of forty-five minutes when I couldn't find my bag even though it was right behind me, we left the airport.

We all hit it off immediately and the drive was fun. When we got to the camp, the first thing we saw was a guy standing in the back of his pickup truck singing "Born to Run" to two other people through a portable karaoke machine. I was in heaven.

Although, thanks to my family, I was certainly used to camping, this was nothing like what I'd experienced in the past. It was crazy hot during the day and freezing at night. We had no running water. The guys had packed a ton of bottles for drinking and for the occasional attempt at an armpit wash. I gave myself a little pat on the back for remembering to pack some Always feminine wipes since Ira had warned me that the shower situation was grim. I also took long walks to the outhouse every day. There was no way I was going number two in an RV.

I always saw something ridiculous when I wandered around. I saw a guy riding his bike completely naked, which seemed both brave and painful. There were "techno" tents set up for raves. One group of guys had built a huge, crazy maze. I wandered in and smoked pot, which I don't do well, then ended up sitting in a corner of the maze until someone came by and led me to the exit.

The second night, one of Ira's friends suggested we do mushrooms. I had never done them before and I was still afraid of drugs. Pot was all I had ever tried and I wanted to keep it that way. As far as I knew, the worst thing alcohol did was make you puke and/or forget stuff. Those were two consequences I was comfortable with. I didn't like the idea of anything that might make me lose complete control and jump off a building or run through a glass door, which is what I was convinced mushrooms would do. That being said, when Ira's friend offered them to me I said "Sure!" and ate a handful. After all, this was the new, spontaneous Sarah. I needed to take mushrooms to get myself to the next level. It was a horrible, horrible idea.

When the mushrooms started to take effect, I began to realize I was in the middle of nowhere with three guys I barely knew, and thousands of other people who were carrying glow sticks that I started to think were actually butcher knives. *What am I doing here? Am I insane?* Too bad I had that thought, because that's when it hit me that I was going insane. Ira looked at me, noticed that things were headed downhill fast, and suggested he and I go back to the RV. He slowly guided me back to our camping spot, reassuring me that once we got there I was going to be okay.

"You're probably just overwhelmed," he told me. "You just need to sit down and take a few deep breaths."

He sat with me in the trailer and tried to get my mind off the fact that I was losing it. He asked me lots of questions about myself but all I could think about was what camping was like when I was growing up. I didn't understand why it had to be so different now, other than the fact that my mom fed me biscuits and gravy rather than hallucinogens.

He listened while I talked about how much my family liked to go camping, and how there was an unspoken competition among them all about who had the better camping trailer. I was definitely not making sense, because Ira thought I meant that my family actually held an annual trailer competition. I was frustrated at how white trash that sounded, but I couldn't fix it. I was just a floating mouth that was babbling while underneath it all my brain was reeling with images of me in a straitjacket.

I pictured my mom telling people what kind of potential I'd had before I lost my mind. People would agree and say it was sad I allowed myself to be pulled into the world of drugs.

"I thought she was smarter than that, but I guess I was wrong," she'd sigh as she completed the paperwork to have me committed.

Ira sat with me all night until eventually the mushrooms wore off. I had curled up on the sad little RV bed and he had curled up next to me. When I woke up in the morning I was relieved to figure out that nothing had happened between us, and that I was sane.

I rolled over and looked at him. He was wide awake. "I think I'll just stick to drinking for the rest of the trip," I announced.

That night his friends suggested we do ecstasy. Jesus, had nobody seen what had happened to me the night before?

"I can't do any more drugs," I told them.

"It's okay, I promise. Nobody I know has ever had a bad trip on ecstasy," his friend urged.

"Has anyone you know ever had a bad trip on mushrooms?" I asked.

"Totally, all the time."

"Thanks for the heads-up on that last night."

His other friend piped in. "Tonight is when they actually

'burn the man.' It's the big event. Everyone will be on E. You have to do it!"

"She doesn't have to." Ira grabbed my hand. "You don't have to."

"Are *you* going to?" I asked him.

"Yeah."

"Then so am I," I said. I figured if the conservative Jewish guy was doing it, I should, too.

Aside from the burning-of-the-man ceremony, it was costume night. I dropped a hit of ecstasy and headed out to the big gathering place wearing a teal prom dress and no shoes. I barely recognized who I was, but felt a huge sense of pride that I was once again stepping so far out of my comfort zone.

Ira's friend was right. Doing ecstasy was a blast. I danced around in circles and laughed and talked to complete strangers. I marveled at how good the air felt. At one point I had wandered off from the group. I plopped down by some guy who immediately started talking to me.

"What do you do?" he asked.

"I'm a bartender," I replied. I was also a waitress, but bartender sounded more impressive.

"Cool. How old are you?" he asked.

"Almost twenty-five!" I said excitedly. I loved ecstasy. This was the first time that I'd been excited about turning twenty-five.

"Why are you almost twenty-five and just a bartender?"

I stared at him for a second, or maybe it was ten minutes. I felt like someone was letting the air out of my big new balloon.

"I don't know." *Shit, why am I just a bartender?* I felt myself start to panic.

We sat there in silence for a moment, then I stood up and walked away.

I heard him try to call after me but I kept going. I didn't want to let what he said ruin my night. I decided that I was becoming stronger and more independent—that, or it was just really good ecstasy.

I spotted Ira standing with the other guys and walked up to them. I was wearing a prom dress, and now I had found my date.

"There you are!" he said with a huge smile. "Are you having fun?"

"I'm having the best time."

I meant it. Bad trip and rude guy aside, the past few days had been fantastic. I was really, really starting to like Ira.

When we returned to L.A., our relationship quickly escalated to full-on boyfriend and girlfriend. I was crazy about him, and he was crazy about me. It also turned out he was a lightweight. But I decided it was cute that he got a buzz off one Stoli Vanilla and ginger ale. It was different from how I felt when I was with Kevin. Ira didn't judge me or make me feel self-conscious. I could be goofy, or I could be drunk, and he didn't roll his eyes at me either way. He seemed to like the real me. So I wanted to like the real him.

I remember once going out for Mexican food with him. He ordered a blended strawberry margarita. Normally that kind of behavior would prompt me to say, "Do you crave strawberries when you're on your period?" but with Ira I held my tongue. He was an aspiring writer. He wanted to write plays and TV shows and did really adult things like stay home during the week when he was working on a project, but he managed to stay fun. I figured maybe he had his shit together because he didn't drink five tequilas on the rocks on a Tuesday night. In solidarity, I ordered a frozen strawberry margarita, too. It was a very loving and adult move for me.

I started to think that maybe this relationship was going to be a good influence on me. I had been panicking for months that my career hadn't taken off yet. I wasn't sure if I wanted a family . . . but the career, I knew that was what I wanted. Now I was with someone who seemed to know how to make things happen for himself, and maybe that would rub off on me.

A couple of months into my relationship with Ira, I got an email from Marc. It was the first I'd heard back since sending him that email about the commercial. My heart skipped a beat when I saw his name, and my hands shook a little as I read the email. It said that he was going to be in L.A. for two nights and he wanted to get together. I felt like I was doing something wrong even reading the email, but I had to see him.

After hours of laboring over how to handle it, I settled on talking to Ira about Marc's visit. I decided that if I told him what was going on, it was okay for me to do it. I'd see Marc, I'd tell him that I had a boyfriend, and we'd just have a nice meal as friends. I was in an adult relationship and this was an adult situation that needed to be handled with an adult attitude. I shoved aside the urge to lie about the whole thing, meet Marc in a hotel, and fuck his brains out.

Ira handled the conversation pretty well. He said that if I wanted to see Marc then I should see him. He acted tough, but I could tell that it was bothering him. To make matters worse, the same night that I was going to be able to see Marc, Ira and I had plans to go to a friend's party.

"If that's the only night you can see him, I can just go to

the party by myself," he said graciously. "No problem!" But the look on his face told me it was a problem.

As I was getting ready to meet Marc, I felt like I was going to throw up. I was nervous and excited and guilty. When I started to obsess about what to wear, I realized that seeing him was a bad idea. I obviously had some unsettled feelings for him. One drink and I might end up convincing myself it wouldn't be cheating if he just went down on me for a few minutes.

If I wanted the relationship with Ira to work I was going to need to let this night go. I called Marc, told him I was sorry that I couldn't make dinner, and drove to meet my boyfriend at the birthday party. The look of relief on Ira's face when I walked in the door was all I needed to know that I had made the right decision.

For several years of my life I dreaded every December, knowing I'd have to go home for Christmas and try to make it seem like things were great in Los Angeles. Maybe they *were* okay; I wouldn't know because I had set my expectations so high for when I'd be doing what. All I knew was that I didn't want my family to think I'd made a bad decision. And I didn't want to have to run into any of the annoying, pissy girls I went to high school with in Wal-Mart and answer their barrage of questions.

"Why are you living in California if all you're doing is serving Jack-and-Cokes?" the last girl I'd run into had asked.

"Well, I'm just doing that for now. You have to have a night job so you can go to auditions and stuff," I said in an attempt to defend myself.

"Well, why don't you forget about that little fantasy of

yours and come back! You can get a job easily. They have bars here, you know!"

"I know, your husband is in one every night," I said with a smile and walked off. "Oh, and if you're looking for the Slim-Fast, try aisle five." I didn't actually say that last part, but I wish I had. I was just trying to impress you, the reader.

My birthday is also in December. The year I was with Ira I spent Christmas in Arkansas but came home in time to spend my twenty-fifth birthday with him. When it struck midnight and it was officially my birthday, Ira lit up. He smiled and kissed me and told me happy birthday. I started crying.

"Oh my God, you're crying! Oh, shit, what did I do? Should I leave?"

Ira was three years older than me, but I was his first real girlfriend. He had no idea how to handle female emotions.

"You didn't do anything!" I cried. "You're perfect! It's just—I'm such a loser. I'm twenty-five and I have to wear a vest and a bow tie to work every day. I can't believe you're even with me."

Ira held me and told me how silly I was.

"Twenty-five is so young, Sarah. You don't have to have everything figured out yet."

"You have everything figured out. I bet you even did when you were my age."

"I don't have anything figured out, except that I love you."

A huge sense of relief washed over me. His words made me smile, so I allowed my boyfriend to make me feel better. He took me to dinner that night at the Palm, which is a famous old restaurant in Hollywood. It was pretty expensive in comparison to places I had been eating at with my Mirabelle money. I couldn't believe when you ordered a steak all you got was the steak. In Arkansas that would have come with a baked potato, vegetable, AND you could add a house salad for a dollar. Here you had to order all of the sides separately and they were like eight dollars each. I ordered up a storm and reminded myself to tell my grandpa how *not* cheap Ira was—at least for that night. Usually he was actually kind of cheap.

There was a several-week phase that he stayed home every night to work on something, so we barely saw each other. He preferred I didn't sleep over, so that he didn't "lose focus." So I went out with my friends more than I had in a while. I drank lots, then when he'd ask me about my night I'd tell him I'd gotten home early and had only had a couple of drinks. I appreciated that he worked hard. I worked hard at trying to get my career going, too. But I've always believed you also have to have fun. Otherwise what's the point? Maybe Ira didn't know how to do both. He seemed to go to such an extreme when in "work mode." And I felt really left out.

Whatever my insecurities were, they were magnified by the feeling that I wasn't good enough or doing enough. Now it was like it felt with Kevin, but this time the guy wasn't judging me. I was judging myself.

Once again I wasn't the same person when I was with my boyfriend as I was when I was without him. Before, I'd stay over and I would wake up and make breakfast for him and watch TV with him and feel that "couple" thing that I assumed was like being married. If marriage were as simple as bacon and eggs and a *Friends* rerun, I'd be a fucking expert. But now I felt shut out and I was getting restless. I decided that I didn't know what I was thinking before, but twenty-five was way too young to be tied down.

We broke up on July 2. Don't ask why I remember that. I thought it was an incredibly romantic split because we both cried. A couple of days later I decided I needed to have fun so I went to Chris Franjola's annual July Fourth party. This party was a mess. It was at his apartment complex pool—which is always gross. There was a ton of drinking, bad cheese dip, and lots of good hair band music. For some reason when Chris and his roommate thought of July Fourth, they thought of Mötley Crüe. Normally I'd be really on board with that, but since Mötley Crüe was the band Ira and I had bonded over, the sound of Vince Neil's voice devastated me. "Don't Go Away Mad" still does. That's just a good fucking song.

I hadn't told many people that we'd broken up. I don't always like to talk about stuff right away. I find it easier to keep shit to myself so that I can control when difficult subjects surface. When you tell people you're going through something, they tend to follow up by asking how you're dealing with that something. If you were having a good day on said subject, then their question just ruined it. The words "How are you?" can pack a mean punch.

Being newly single can quickly go from the feeling of "Fuck yeah" to "Oh, fuck" after a handful of drinks. Suddenly I was finding myself not having the fun I usually had at a party. If anybody kissed or held hands I wanted to drown them in the sad, dirty pool. If anybody wanted to know where Ira was, I found myself breaking my own rules and spilling my guts about our breakup, which was a buzzkill for them and screwed up any future party invites for me.

When the speakers started blaring "Girls, Girls, Girls" my emotions took over.

I stumbled to the street, not sober, to find my car. *I should probably go talk to Ira,* I thought. I was wearing a bikini and a wrap around my waist, and it was 9 P.M., but I didn't have enough time to change my clothes and fix my life at the same time.

I ran into this guy Zack, who I worked with at Mirabelle. He was a cute Southern guy who I always liked flirting with.

"Where you goin' darlin'?" he asked.

I mumbled something along the lines of "Do you think I'm pretty?" then we made out. I've always been a sucker for a guy with a Southern accent.

I realized what I was doing about the same time his hand was headed down my pants. Getting fingered by a co-worker on the street while wearing a bikini was probably not going to make me feel better. I wiggled out of his grasp and managed to get in my car without further groping.

"Are you sure you should be driving?" Zack yelled through the window.

"I should definitely not be," I slurred, and then I got out and called a taxi, which I still have on speed dial.

There was no time to sober up. All I could think was: *I have to find Ira, he's my soul mate. Oh my God, how didn't I see that before? It was meant to be.* I figured he was at his apartment working on a script—it was the Fourth of July, after all.

On the way to his place, I had a really good idea: *Flowers. Who doesn't love flowers?* I marveled at my own genius. I asked the taxi driver, who had already suggested to me that I just go home rather than to my ex-boyfriend's house, to make a quick stop at a Ralph's grocery store. He reluctantly obliged. I was dead set on getting some roses to take with me. I would explain to Ira that I was silly to think I needed to be single, and that a relationship with him, no matter how stagnant, was exactly what I wanted. After all, *he* wasn't boring; *I* just needed to settle down. *I'm fucking twenty-five,* I reminded myself. *It's time to get my shit together.*

I walked into Ralph's in my bikini. My eyes were red and blurry with tears, so I asked someone where the flowers were. I was standing right next to them.

"Great, thanks. Now just show me where the checkout lane is and I'll be on my way."

When the cab pulled up to Ira's apartment I noticed that all the lights were off. I asked the driver to wait for me. He rolled his eyes and said, "Okay, but I can't watch." Then he looked away. That should have been my first hint.

I hoped Ira wasn't in bed. I had practiced my speech on the way over, and I'd hate for the only person ever to hear it to be Akim, the taxi driver. Several knocks on the door and I started to panic. Shit, he was asleep. I looked at my cellphone to check the time. Ten o'clock. Why was he in bed so early?

*Oh, maybe he's out,* I realized. He'd probably decided to have some fun on the Fourth and let his writing take a day off. Good for him! *Maybe if he'd done that with me we wouldn't be in this mess.*

Ira was so adult that he actually had a nice apartment. It was one of the fancy ones with a front *and* back door, something I couldn't afford yet. I decided that since he wasn't home, his back porch was a good location to leave the roses. I didn't have a pen but I figured, *No need for a note, he'll know who they're from.*

I played out the whole scenario in my head. Ira was at a disappointing party. He would have seen couples, just like I had. He'd be feeling sad and missing me, just like I had him. He would decide "fuck it" and have two apple martinis instead of one. Feeling pretty buzzed, he wouldn't be able to take the party anymore so he'd call a cab and go home. He'd go in through the back door—he never did—but in this case he would because that's where my roses were. *He'll just know.*

Akim drove me home, pretending the whole time to agree I had handled this whole thing perfectly. He was polite enough to realize the damage was done, so why make me feel worse? I also had given him a huge tip.

The next morning I woke up and my head hurt. I don't know if it hurt from the alcohol, the crying, or both. I walked into the bathroom to get some aspirin and noticed I was still in my bikini. I had a quick flashback to leaving the roses. I grabbed my phone to make sure I hadn't missed a call. I had not.

Thoughts of what he might have done the night before flooded my head. Did he hook up with a girl? Did he stay out late and he's still asleep? Did he find my roses and now he and his roommate are laughing at me for being so pathetic?

Humiliation washed over me. I don't care how many people say, "Men like flowers too!" There's no excuse for a girl leaving a guy roses. A simple phone call would have been sufficient if I had wanted to talk.

I rolled out of bed and drove in a panic to his apartment, still wearing the bikini. That could not have been good. It was still damp from the pool. I definitely remembered reading something in health class about that causing female issues. But I didn't have time to change once again. I realized that Ira might not have come home the night before, or maybe he used the front door. My roses might still be on the back step. I could go get them, take them away without his ever knowing I had left them, and call him that night like a reasonable human being.

I pulled up to the street behind Ira's place because from there I could get a clear shot of his back porch. I had figured that out at a different low point in our relationship. I peered through my window and saw that the roses were gone. *Fuck me in the face.*

He'd come home. He'd gotten the roses. And he hadn't called.

The responsible girl who thought Ira might be the right guy tried to get through to the irresponsible girl who thought he was boring, but she had shown up a little too late.

I looked down at my bikini bottom and figured the damage was already done. I picked up my phone and called Zack. He answered. I drove right over to his house to finish what we had started on the street the night before.

Forget growing up. I was right where I belonged.

## REALLY BAD HAIR DAY

I decided that since I was single I could finally get laser-focused on my career. I entered a stand-up competition that was sponsored by Comedy Central. After passing the first level I had to perform a five-minute set at the Hollywood Improv. I didn't end up winning the competition, but Comedy Central still put me on *Premium Blend,* a stand-up show featuring a few comics at a time. I felt like I was finally getting a real break. I wondered if Ira had heard that things were going so great for me.

The competition led to me getting my first big agent at one of the best agencies in town and up to that point I had only auditioned for commercials. I was ecstatic at the idea that now I had an agent who could get me auditions for real television shows.

I was still thinking about Ira a lot but this new development made me feel stronger. I was convinced these things wouldn't be happening if I was still with him. It was when I was alone that I succeeded the most. I needed to remember to do things opposite of the "traditional" way. Get my career settled. Make a life for myself. Depend on nobody. Stand on my own two feet and don't even think about having a relationship until that is all set in stone. I had a plan.

My agent set up a showcase (audition) for me for the Montreal comedy festival, Just for Laughs. That was where all the comics I knew wanted to go. It could help launch your career. He knew that I hadn't been doing stand-up long but he was sure this was going to be a good move for me. I wasn't sure I was ready, but I figured since he was an agent he knew more than I did.

The showcase was on a Thursday night at the Hollywood Improv. I was told I was supposed to do ten minutes of material, which was exactly what I had accumulated so far.

When I got to the club I saw a huge line outside. The sign was lit up with the name Drew Carey. I got butterflies. *What a big night.*

I was the last comedian to go up before Drew Carey. I walked up, nervous but confident.

"If you guys are drinking tonight, please don't drive," I started. The audience just looked at me, but that was okay since I hadn't gotten to the punch line yet.

"They have this new device that they put on your ignition. You breathe into it, and if it detects alcohol on your breath, your car won't start. Brutal, right? But wouldn't it be awesome if they could put something like that on my cellphone?"

The sound of dead fucking silence resonated through my body. My knees felt weak. I didn't understand what had happened; that exact same joke had killed when I did it before for the Comedy Central thing. *Did they not hear the punch line?*

I didn't really know what the hell was going on at the time, but I do now. Those people were there to see Drew Carey. They didn't give a shit about me in my light blue tank top with my big platform shoes rambling on about how I liked to drink and dial.

I was way too new at stand-up to have any idea how to handle the situation so I just plowed through my jokes, not that I needed to pause for laughter anyway, and said good night.

As I walked away from the microphone, down the steps, and off the stage, I noticed that the emcee wasn't passing me from the other direction. He was nowhere to be seen and the stage was completely empty. Now I really didn't know what to do, so I kept going. I certainly wasn't going to walk back onstage to the packed crowd of annoyed Drew Carey fans. I felt like they wanted to hurt me.

After at least a minute of dead silence and a crowd of confused faces, the emcee blew past me near the doorway and muttered something that sounded angry. The reality of what a disaster this night had been started to sink in. I knew my agent would be looking for me so I ran and hid in the bathroom. I locked the stall and cried. It was a scene from one of those Lifetime movies I like so much.

After an hour I figured the coast was clear so I headed out of the bathroom and out of the club. I managed to avoid everybody except the emcee.

"What the fuck was that?" he asked.

"What?" I asked back, defensively.

"You had like three minutes left onstage. You don't get offstage when the emcee isn't even in the room," he scolded me.

I didn't bother to fight back. He was right. I felt defeated. I felt humiliated. I felt like I had no idea what the hell I was doing. "I'm really sorry," I mumbled, then I left. Right as I got to my car, my platform wedge gave out and I went flying face-first to the pavement.

"That's about right," I said out loud.

I got in my car, picked the gravel out of my hands, and drove back to my apartment.

I wasn't sure how much damage I'd done to my future, but my agent seemed to brush it off. "It was too early for you to be auditioning for the festival. No big deal . . ." That was pretty much his response.

Even though he seemed okay with what had happened, I was not. I had thought that things were taking off for me, but now it felt like none of the good things from the past couple of months had even happened. I wondered if it was over before it really started. I obviously didn't know how to handle myself in the comedy world, plus the idea of doing stand-up again made me cringe. I thought that maybe the times before when I'd done really well were a fluke, and what happened at the Improv was the reality. Too bad the me then couldn't talk to the me now, who knows one bad night is just that. It doesn't wipe out all of your good ones.

A week later, I got my first audition for a TV show. I spent a ton of time working on my lines and preparing for the audition. I felt really confident going in. Keep in mind, I felt confident that night at the Improv, too.

The day of the audition it was pouring rain. I drove to

Fox studios and proudly handed them my ID. The guard at the gate directed me to where I was to park, then showed me where my final destination was. The two looked really far away from each other, but I've never been good at reading maps. I parked as directed and headed to my audition in the rain. I had an umbrella but when the wind is blowing at forty miles an hour, they don't help much.

I had read a map correctly for once; the building I was going to *was* really far from my parking spot. I noted that spots closer to the building were marked RESERVED and fantasized about the day I'd be the lead on a sitcom and would get to pull right up into one of those spots. It wouldn't say RESERVED, though. It would say SARAH COLONNA.

When I finally got to where I was going I was relieved to see that the other girls were in the same shape that I was in: sopping wet. I signed in and waited anxiously to be called to see the casting director.

The audition was over in minutes. I read the scene twice and the casting director smiled and told me I did a great job. He shook my hand and thanked me for coming in. I remembered that my acting teacher said that you never know what it means if your audition goes quickly.

"It can be a good thing. If they give you some direction and you take it, then they've seen what they need to see."

That casting director had given me direction, and I knew that I had taken it. I didn't mind the rain or the walk back to my car because I felt great. Nobody is harder on me than I am, so if I felt I'd done a good job that meant that I had. I didn't know how it all worked, but I sat in my car and prayed that I got the part. Maybe I sucked at the showcase the other night because I wasn't supposed to go to Montreal. I was supposed to be in town so I could get this job. Maybe stand-up wasn't my thing as much as acting.

Later that day my phone rang and I saw that it was my agent's number. *This could be the call,* I thought.

"Hello?" I answered excitedly.

"Hey, it's Ron."

"Hey! What's up?"

"How'd it go today?" he asked.

He was messing with me. He wanted to drag out the good news!

"Good. Really good. I think he liked me. . . ."

"Hmmmm. All right. Well, we just got a call from him. I don't want you to get upset, but he wasn't quite as positive."

Or he was trying to find a nice way to tell me to move back to Arkansas.

I was silent for a minute. "Well, okay then. What did he say?"

"He said you were kind of a mess. That you looked like the wind just blew you in. He was worried about your appearance."

My appearance? I'm not always well put together, but I certainly am when I need to be and that day I needed to be.

"Well, the wind kind of did blow me in. It was pouring rain and I had to park seventeen miles from the building."

"Calm down, I just wanted to ask you what happened. . . ."

"But everyone looked like that. I mean, my hair was wet but I wasn't in rags. I didn't have BO. I just had to walk there during a tornado, no big deal!"

"He just seemed upset about it. Look, it's the first time

he met you and we've really talked you up. Maybe he's just being really hard on you or had weird expectations."

"Did he say anything about my acting?" I asked.

"No, not a word. He just told us your hair was a mess. That was his feedback."

I was silent.

"Don't sweat this. It sounds like he's got a stick up his ass today. I'll touch base with you later," Ron said. We hung up.

I immediately called my friend Liz. She and her husband, Brandon, were my college friends who had moved out to California. She was working at a talent agency and I thought maybe she knew something about this casting director.

"Oh my God, him?" she asked. "He's just a bitchy queen. That has nothing to do with you. What did he say about your acting?"

"Not a word. I spent all of this time preparing for the audition and all he cared about was that my hair was messy," I told her. "I guess I should have worn a cap."

Even though I laughed the incident off, my ego took a huge beating. I wasn't feeling very confident about my life decisions. And I wasn't feeling very talented. The phone call I got from my agency a few weeks later didn't help.

"Hello?" I answered.

"Hey, it's Peter."

"Oh, hey Peter." I was confused. He worked with Ron but he never called me.

"Listen, I've been trying to get you in the door with casting directors and it's just not working. Nobody has ever heard of you and you don't have any credits to help me sell you. We're just gonna part ways. Good luck down the road." He said it all in one breath and with very little compassion.

"Hey, Peter? Just one thing . . ."

"What?" he sounded like he was being forced at gunpoint to listen to what I had to say.

"You guys knew I had no credits. You came to me. I just want that to be clear. Maybe it was a mistake, but please don't talk to me like I've been a burden."

Don't be too impressed. I cried for about an hour after that. I went straight to my bedroom and curled up in a ball. The sports editor's daughter in me felt like this was strike three, and I was out.

# LIAR, LIAR, PANTS ON FIRE

I spent the next year and a half dating somebody that I didn't really like. I liked him as a friend, I liked him as a person, but as a boyfriend he kind of sucked. He was a comic, so knowing that Ira would hear about it and figure out that I had moved on and was doing great motivated me to keep things going with Marvin.

Marvin was a huge flirt. He had a way of making a girl feel special, which—if you are slow on the uptake—is what girls want. Unfortunately he didn't discriminate, so I spent most of our relationship encountering women who were "shocked" to meet Marvin's girlfriend since they were "sure he was single!" In some ways his flirtatious nature probably kept us together past the point that we should have been; I was so busy fighting for my new boyfriend's attention that I didn't have time to think about the fact that I was still hung up on my ex.

I tried a few times to get Marvin to go by his real name, which was Greg. Greg was a nice normal name and Marvin was his shitty middle name. For some reason he preferred it. I'm not sure what the deal is with me dating guys who like to go by ridiculous names. He insisted that the name Marvin was more original than Greg. I explained to him that sometimes things that seem original only seem original because everyone else is smart enough not to use them.

The day that he asked me to move in with him was the day that I knew it was about to end. At the time I was living with a girl named Nicky and he was living with a guy named David. Nicky was lots of fun to live with, but she was messy. Sometimes she'd get up from the couch and would leave behind crumbs when she hadn't even been eating. She put food wrappers in the bathroom trash, which really grosses me out. One should always know the difference between kitchen and bathroom garbage. I'm also certain that her unreasonable love for cigarettes is how my cat developed asthma. The asthma was something that I discovered after weeks of listening to him wheeze. I assumed it was a hairball so I continued to give him remedies that pet stores and the Internet told me to. When things didn't get any better I took him to the vet, who diagnosed his condition and informed me that my cat would need a cortisone shot every few months to keep it under control. I cursed Neil and his audacity to die and leave me with an asthmatic cat.

So it was after about a year of dating that Marvin started looking for an apartment for us. I told him that I wanted to get my own place.

"But we've been talking about this for months. We knew

both of our leases were going to be up. You said you'd want to move in together," he said.

"No, I said I *probably* wanted to move in together," I shot back.

"That's no excuse. I didn't look for a new roommate. Now my roommate is moving in with his girlfriend and I won't have a roommate anymore. This is a bad time to change your mind."

"Well needing a roommate is no reason to live together!" I yelled.

"I wouldn't need a roommate now if you hadn't been telling me for months that you were going to be my roommate!"

His mind was like a steel trap. And I was sick of hearing the word *roommate*.

"Fine," I replied. "Fine. I screwed up. I thought I'd be ready to move in with you but I'm not. I've never lived by myself and I think it's really important that I do that before I live with a man. I need to know that kind of independence." I'd read that in a self-help book that I had browsed through in a store but had never purchased.

We didn't break up, but Marvin was pissed off that he had taken the leap of asking me to move in with him and had been shot down. I couldn't really understand what the big deal was. I was still his girlfriend, after all—he was getting his cake and eating it, too. It wasn't until I hit my early thirties and had to break up with a guy who I was very much in love with because he had no interest in living with me, that I finally felt Marvin's pain.

I found my own place. The day I moved in, he refused to help. I had to pay movers with the two hundred dollars I had left to my name. While I unpacked the tons of boxes all by my fucking self even though I had a fucking boyfriend, I decided I was going to break up with him. Now I was living by myself *and* I was newly single. I wasn't sure if I was supposed to be excited or sad.

Luckily for me, Jackie had just left her husband, although I'm not sure she was legally married anyway because they had gotten married in Mexico after knowing each other for three weeks. Now she needed a place to stay. She thought she was imposing, since I had just gotten my own place for the first time in my life. She was not. I wanted the company and if she slept on the couch I would most likely not need a night-light; I have never recovered from watching the movie *Cujo*. That dog was mean.

Jackie and I had met when we worked together at Mirabelle. I was now bartending at a place called Formosa, and she was working at a really nice restaurant on Sunset Boulevard. Almost every day she'd come home with an expensive bottle of wine. It didn't matter if it was 1 P.M. or 9 P.M.; we'd drink it. If we both had a whole day and night off, we were drunk before 5 P.M. and asleep by 10 P.M. I was taking huge steps backward, and I was having a blast.

I decided I'd get my shit together when she found her own place; it didn't seem worth it to try while she was staying with me. I also told myself she really needed me since her marriage had crumbled. It would have been selfish to focus on my own life.

When the day came that she actually did find her own apartment, I was bummed. There was no way I'd be able to live alone and keep acting the way I'd been acting. I'd feel too guilty and/or end up choking on my own vomit.

Since I was alone again, I figured I should be productive. I hadn't been doing much stand-up since the Drew Carey incident. I'd gone to a couple of coffee shops or small bars to do sets, but I was too scared to go anywhere with a real paying crowd that might despise me. I decided to try to change that one day after I got a card in the mail from my mom.

She and I had had a conversation during which I broke down and cried. I didn't often do that with her. In fact, the only other time I can really think of was when I later had to break up with the guy who didn't want to live with me. I tended to keep my chin up so she didn't worry. But for some reason during this particular conversation, when she asked how I was doing I couldn't just say "fine." I was disappointed that I was on the verge of turning thirty and was still bartending. I started to really consider that I'd made a huge mistake moving to L.A. and that I had missed my opportunity to stay in Arkansas and have several children with a guy I hated.

The card that she sent a few days after that conversation was simple and sweet. It said that she was proud of me and supported me. It said not to ever doubt what I wanted to do with my life. It arrived when I needed it the most.

I decided to get myself booked on a show at the Improv. I figured if I was really going to get back into stand-up I had to start there. I needed to conquer my fear of that place. I told myself that if it didn't go well, it didn't matter. All that did matter was that I got up there.

When I walked into the Improv, I immediately ordered a drink. I'm not one of those people who refuse to perform with alcohol in them. In fact, I prefer it. Jackie had come with me, so I bought her a drink and within a few minutes we were on our second round. I had huge butterflies in my stomach. I still always have a little bit of nerves when I perform, but that's something I believe in. I think if you get *too* comfortable you might stop trying.

When I got onstage and took the microphone I just assumed everyone could see my hands shaking.

"If you guys are drinking, please don't drive . . . ," I began. I figured if I was going to start over, I should really start over. Plus I hadn't spent much time performing, so thus far that was my best opening joke.

"Too bad they can't put one of those on my phone, so that when I get home at two in the morning and it detects alcohol on my breath, it just shuts off—before I call every man that I know."

The audience laughed. They laughed a lot. Side note: I know it isn't that funny now, but this was before texting took over and when drunk dialing was hugely popular. I spotted Jackie and she gave me a huge smile.

I was relieved that it went well because if it hadn't I probably would have been set back another eleven months. I had totally lied to myself earlier. "It's brave that you even got up there" is just what people say when they think you suck.

I finally got some momentum back and started getting booked in commercials again. Most important, I was able to quit the side job I'd been doing as a secret shopper for hotels. It didn't pay much and I kept it longer than I needed to, but I have incredible guilt about turning down any way to make money when I need it. I'm actually surprised I never guilted myself into stripping.

The hotel job sucked. Basically I had to call amazing places like the Four Seasons in Maui and make a fake reservation, all the while filling out a check sheet indicating whether the reservation agent was meeting the criteria they were supposed to meet. I had to record the conversations, which meant I had to have my apartment as quiet as possible, which meant that I couldn't even turn on a fan in the middle of July. I didn't have air-conditioning—living alone was pretty expensive so I could only afford an apartment with very few perks, like a working shower. Aside from an all-new *General Hospital,* having a fan on was the highlight of my day and that stupid job wouldn't allow me to do even that. It was also really depressing to have reservation agents describe to me the amenities and grounds of lavish hotels that I didn't think I'd ever be able to afford to stay in, as I sat Indian-style on the floor of my apartment in the sun.

I got another agent for television stuff, an older man named Sal who was well liked around town but not all that powerful. I didn't really care; I just wanted someone to believe in me and I considered the fact that he wasn't a snotty asshole a bonus. I started getting work on a hidden-camera show on the Sci-Fi channel. Geeky guys who watched that channel and came into the bar would recognize me from the show. They seemed really disappointed to figure out that I was also a bartender. People seem to think if you're on TV you should be making enough money that you don't have to keep a day job. That's not the case. I didn't really care—with more work coming, I finally felt like there was light at the end of the tunnel.

Just when I was starting to feel good about myself I met Nico. He had a really deep voice and a lean body. I later caught on that his lean body may or may not have been from a cocaine addiction. He was an actor who was having a tough time finding work, but had been successful a few years earlier. He became successful again after we quit seeing each other. I have great timing.

Nico was the type of guy who made me trip over nothing and drop things. His existence at the bar cost my boss a lot in replacement glassware. The first time I went home with him I had sex with him—even though I had promised myself that I wouldn't. I wanted to feel sexy our first time and I didn't in my dirty black jeans and hair that smelled like Chinese food. Formosa serves Chinese food—I didn't just randomly carry that scent.

Nico lived right down the street, so he always walked to the bar. That night he suggested I come over and go with him to take his dogs for a walk. I thought it was just a cute way to get me to his place, but we really did take his dogs for a walk. As if I didn't find him sexy enough already, now I got to watch him care for these two adorable dogs that he obviously loved so much. As we walked he told me a story about how one of them had gotten really sick and he ended up paying over fifty thousand dollars in vet bills to get him well again. I was impressed that he'd spend that kind of money to save an animal, but I was more impressed that at one point he had an extra fifty grand lying around. We stopped to let his dogs pee under a streetlight and he turned and planted a big kiss on me. I was taken aback a little at first. He was so good-looking. It didn't make sense that he'd pick me, the bartender at his local spot who sometimes scared the shit out of innocent people on a hidden-camera show.

Nico had a lot of tattoos, one of them being an ex-girlfriend's name. I don't know how I was able to see my way to his bedroom with all the red flags waving. But on top of the dark hair and the scruffy face, he held a couple of my other weaknesses: upper-arm tattoos and a love for cigarettes. I don't really like kissing smokers—I just like watching hot guys smoke. Unfortunately it's rude to have sex with a smoker without kissing him, so sometimes I have to make the sacrifice. After we had sex that night, I slept over and we had a blast. I always laughed when I was with him, which was just another reason I was so attracted to him. He was almost forty and I was in my late twenties. Although he drank like a fish, I had the illusion that he was a grown-up and I thought we could have an amazing life together. He could teach me about "the business" and I could teach him about popular new drinks.

For a while we hooked up on and off. For the most part, I kept other aspects of my life quiet around him. I felt like he'd worked in the industry enough and anything I was doing would seem silly to him.

The day after a crappy showcase for another comedy festival, I had to cater some awful outdoor corporate party down by the airport. Another side job—I told you I don't know how to turn down work. This was a particularly shitty party with a barbecue theme on a particularly shitty day. I was walking back to my car with lemonade all over my white shirt and tri-tip on my pants, trying to figure out if catering was really worth the sixty-four extra dollars I had made that day. I decided it was not, and that it would be my last shift. It was almost as liberating as quitting the phone call job.

I felt my phone vibrating in my apron, and looked down to see that "N" was calling me. I hadn't put Nico's full name in my phone because I thought just using an initial created distance between us. I was really working on not getting my heart broken, and I was nailing it. Since I was pretty sure he'd never called me before 10 P.M., I got so excited that I tripped over a speed bump in the parking lot.

"Hello?" I panted oh so casually as I wiped the blood off my forehead.

"Hey, it's Nico."

"Hey, it's Sarah," I said.

"What's that noise—are you at the airport?"

"A plane almost landed on me. I'm by the airport."

"Oh. You going somewhere?"

I was supposed to bartend that night. If I didn't tell him the truth I'd probably have to actually go out of town. "No, I'm just in that area. I'm catering an amazing party."

"You have another job that I didn't know about?"

"Yeah."

"Well, it sounds awful."

"It is. But I'm quitting after today. I need to focus on my bartending career."

He laughed. I felt relieved.

"I was just wondering how the show went. You said it was for a festival, seemed like a big deal."

I was surprised he retained that much of our conversation. "It was great!" I lied. The truth was that it was "fine," not "great," but I didn't want him to think I sucked at stand-up.

I hoped that daytime phone call might be the start of something serious, but it wasn't. We continued to see each other off and on for a couple of months, but I think we only went on one real date, and even that was at a bar.

One day a new girl was sitting in a booth at Formosa

with him. They seemed really close, too close. He didn't pay much attention to me and I started to feel like I was going to cry, or at least pass out. Before he left he walked over and said goodbye to me, to which I responded "yep" without even looking at him. *Ha! I showed him.*

After leaving with that girl, he had the balls to call me later that night. I'd had about fourteen drinks, so I answered, ready to tell him where to go.

"Before you say anything, just listen. I had to walk her home because she was a mess. I did used to go out with her, but she's crazy. Nothing happened."

"Perfect, that explains why you sat with her all night and acted like I was in quarantine," I slurred. I have zero ability to hide my feelings when I've been drinking. Actually I can't even do that sober.

"I haven't seen her in a long time. I was just being polite. I felt like if I introduced you to her she'd say something stupid. She really is crazy."

"Who were you being polite to? You weren't being polite to me. You're exactly what Cassie said you are."

Cassie, the eighty-year-old waitress who worked at Formosa with me, had warned me that Nico was a "ladies' man." He and I had laughed about it in the past, but that night I stopped thinking it was funny. Even though it seemed like he was telling the truth, the feeling that I got in my stomach when I saw her walk up to him scared the shit out of me.

"I guess I am," he resigned.

Nico wasn't one to confront an issue, and neither was I. We basically just let it all fizzle after that. Unfortunately that didn't stop him from coming into the bar. It was annoying for two reasons: 1) He would talk to girls that he was obviously trying to pick up right in front of my face; 2) I used to think he came in all of the time to see me, but now it was clear he just liked to drink.

Regardless of who that other slut was, he eventually started coming in with girls that he was definitely dating. Each time I felt like my heart was being ripped out, but I never let him know. One time after a particularly long night of watching him hold court with a stupid-looking blonde, I snapped and texted him a list of five other bars in the area that served Red Bull in a can and carried Stoli, just the way he liked. That text led to a bit of conversation and that led to a few more dogwalks between us. Our reconciliation didn't last long and eventually I was ducked in the passenger seat of Jackie's Honda Civic while we did a drive-by to see if anyone else was parked in his driveway.

"Is that that bitch's car who was in with him last night?" Jackie asked as she turned off her engine.

"Maybe. But maybe it's his car."

"I can get closer. What kind of car does he drive?"

"I have no idea."

"Well that's helpful."

If you don't even know what kind of car the guy you are checking up on drives, the whole drive-by is pointless.

Jackie decided that I needed to cleanse Nico from my system. She believed that he was holding me back from moving on with my life. She insisted that I get rid of anything in my apartment that reminded me of him, take it over to the park I lived next to, and burn it in the garbage. He wasn't really my boyfriend so I didn't have that many things that belonged to him, which depressed me even more. If we'd had a real relationship, I would have had plenty of stuff to burn. We would have had photos together or I would have gone home one morning in one of his T-shirts.

I scrounged up a shirt and jeans that I remembered I had worn on that one date we went on to that one bar. I also grabbed a DVD that Jackie and I had rented and not returned of a bad Jesus movie he was in. We set the jeans and the movie on fire, but I couldn't bring myself to burn the shirt. It was really cute. We stood and watched the flames for what felt like hours.

"How long does it take for a pair of jeans to burn?" I asked Jackie.

"I dunno. I guess a while."

We stood there a while longer.

"Maybe it's bad luck that we're destroying a movie about Jesus," I suggested.

"You're just trying to go back inside. Shut up and be patient."

"My legs are starting to hurt," I complained. "How burned does this stuff have to get?"

"It has to burn beyond recognition, so that you no longer recognize the relationship."

"You made that up. Can we just go in?"

"Shut up. It's almost done. I want you to see this through. You need to let go of this asshole."

"Fine."

We stood there for another hour until the last flame went out, then went back into my apartment to drink the rest of the gallon of wine that was responsible for fueling the whole "burn your stuff" idea in the first place.

I guess I didn't get cleansed by the garbage fire, because I still felt sad. About four drunk nights later, I decided that

I would call him. I picked up my home phone, punched in *67 to block my number from showing up on his caller ID, then dialed his number. He answered. I hung up.

Seconds later my phone rang. I got excited that someone was calling me. I was getting kind of bored at home. *Oh, maybe it's Jackie and she'll want to hang out!*

"Hello?" I answered.

"Sarah?" the deep voice asked.

"Yeah?" *Shit.* "Nico?" My legs went numb. Or I was just so drunk I couldn't feel them. The realization that he was calling me because I just called him and hung up on him crept in. I guess *69 trumps *67. I fucking hate AT&T.

"What do you want?" he asked.

"What do you mean? You called me."

"Didn't you just call me and hang up?"

"Nope," I answered with confidence.

"I think you did."

"I didn't."

"You did. It's fine. Just tell me what you wanted."

"Tell me what you want. You called me."

"Sarah. I just got a call and they hung up. I hit star sixty-nine and you answered. So, you must have called me."

"I did not," I slurred.

"You mean to tell me that someone else just called and hung up on me but when I hit star sixty-nine somehow it dialed your number?"

"Yes. You should definitely call the phone company to get that worked out. Now forgive me for being rude, but I gotta hit the sack." With that I hung up the phone.

I didn't see him around much after that. I think he stopped drinking and got his shit together because the next time I saw him was on a pretty successful TV show. I was sitting on my couch alone—drinking wine with no pants on in the shirt that I had refused to burn—when suddenly I heard his voice. I looked up and saw his face, then jumped up to call Jackie and tell her that I hated myself, but I fumbled and fell face-first off the couch. Even through a television he managed to turn me into a klutz.

## DIRTY THIRTY

Like most women who are single, have no money, and haven't achieved many goals outside of having gotten really good at Beer Pong, the closer I got to thirty, the more I started to freak out. It was similar to when I turned twenty-five but much, much more similar to a nervous breakdown.

My career was still moving forward, but it was a slow progression. I didn't want to give up on my dream, but I couldn't figure out what the trick was to making it happen. I worked hard at getting auditions, at performing, at trying to figure it all out. I was getting some work, but at night I still clocked in at the bar. I was going on twelve years in the restaurant business and my head was about to explode.

There should be a support group for people in the restaurant service industry. Food and cocktail ordering brings out the worst in people, and I'm not talking about the ones doing the serving.

Although I never talked much about marriage, I thought I wanted to do it one day.

I didn't think I wanted kids, but I did close my eyes sometimes and think about my wedding day, just like every other asshole does. As happens to most women at that age, my friends started getting married.

Jen Stewart was a girl I'd known for years. She became roommates with Tilley after she and I had moved out of our two-bedroom. She was a ton of fun. I spent many nights drinking with her and Tilley at a hole in the wall across the street from their place called the Starlight Room. Jen and I were terrible influences on each other. We both liked to try new drinks, so we'd always have at least three different types of liquor a night. I'd forgotten my own rule of not mixing. When I finally figured out that that was why we kept waking up with headaches, we opted to stick to our new favorite drink: the White Russian. That phase also ended when one day Jen and I were complaining about our weight gain and Tilley piped up.

"Maybe it's because you're drinking heavy cream every night, assholes."

We both switched to vodka and soda and never looked back.

Jen also worked at Formosa. She was probably how I got the job, which I didn't figure out until later, when she told me that she was secretly dating the owner, Vince.

Jen had kept her relationship with Vince quiet so that nobody would know why she had the better shifts. Up until she finally told us, everyone at work had just assumed that she had the better shifts because she and Vince were secretly dating.

Jen and Vince got married the fall that I was turning thirty. The wedding was in Santa Barbara, and since I didn't have a "plus one," I opted to share a hotel room with another good friend from work, Joanna. She had just turned thirty, and was also handling it terribly. She was the perfect person to go to a wedding dateless with.

Vince had a really hot friend named Scotty. He was ridiculous-looking, one of those guys that you look at and just think, *Well done, God. Well done.* I think he wanted to be an actor, but it wasn't working out. He was getting some modeling work, but he'd gotten sick of trying and had moved to Florida to become a firefighter. *I know. Now* that's *what a firefighter is supposed to look like,* I thought when I heard he had become one. I imagine that women all over Orlando were committing arson just to get an in-home visit from him.

I joked to Joanna that I was going to have dirty, dirty sex with Scotty at the wedding. I guess I'd joked about it so much that I manifested it, because the night of the wedding I had dirty, dirty sex with Scotty.

I had borrowed a dress from Joanna. I'm not going to lie, I looked fucking good. Scotty told me the second he saw me that he couldn't believe how beautiful I looked.

*Perfect. He wants to hook up with me. He's already throwing bad lines at me.*

I didn't own any thongs yet—I found them highly uncomfortable—but the dress called for one so Joanna was kind enough to lend me a pair of her underwear. Halfway through the night I drunkenly stumbled to the bathroom. I

managed to get my dress up high enough to use the restroom, then halfway through peeing I realized that I still had
the underwear on. Those thongs are tricky, you forget they're
there. I didn't feel like walking around in wet underwear,
and I was too old to tell anybody that I'd peed on myself. So
I wiggled out of the thong and threw it away.

I stumbled back out to the reception and found Joanna.

"Have you seen Scotty?" I asked her.

"Yeah, he's over there dancing with his sunglasses on."

"Great. I'm going to go tell him I'm not wearing panties
and see if that can speed up him putting it in me."

"What do you mean you aren't wearing panties?"

"Oh, so funny. I peed on them, so I had to throw them
away. Don't tell anybody!"

"Sarah, those were my underwear."

"Oh, shit."

"Don't worry," she laughed. "I wasn't going to accept
them back from you anyway. I saw you doing the electric
slide earlier. I decided then that I'd never, ever want to wear
them again."

I wandered over to Scotty to try to tell him that I wasn't
wearing underwear. He was involved in a pretty unwatch-
able version of the chicken dance, so I walked back to find
Joanna. I figured the panty conversation could wait.

Eventually Joanna and I took off to a bar with Scotty
and another friend of Vince's. We were pretty intoxicated
already, got more intoxicated at the bar, and decided to go
back to our hotel to get in the hot tub. Joanna and the other
guy excused themselves from said hot tub when it became
pretty apparent that Scotty and I were going to have sex
in it.

I'm pretty sure I've never felt so proud of having sex

with someone I didn't know that well. When I woke up in the morning and he was in my hotel bed, I thought to myself: *Well done, Sarah. Well done.*

Scotty was supposed to go back to Florida the day after the wedding, but some sort of hurricane emergency kept him in L.A. He asked me if he could stay at my place for a couple of days, until he could get home. I casually said, "Sure," then called and made an appointment for a bikini wax.

I was very much enjoying having Scotty as a sleepover guest. We had lots of sex, and in the morning I'd wake up to find him doing crunches on my living room floor. *Makes sense,* I thought to myself.

The only time we had a tiff in our four-day romance was when he was on the phone with Vince and told him that he was at my place.

"What were you thinking!" I yelled after he hung up. "I don't want him to know we're doing it! Gross!"

"Uh, he's my best friend. He knew we did it the night of his wedding."

"Oh my God, he's my BOSS! Did you tell him about the hot tub?"

"Yes, and the elevator."

"Oh my GOD. This is so humiliating. How can I ever look at him again?"

"He thinks it's awesome. He loves you," Scotty said nonchalantly.

"Oh, that's really . . ." I stopped talking, grabbed his hand, and took him right back to my bedroom.

The night before he was going to get to go back to Florida was his birthday. He had plans with some guys, but before he left for the night I surprised him with a cake that I had made. Yes, I am a horrible cook, but I was feeling very sweet that week, probably because I'd been getting laid every hour on the hour. He cut himself a piece and ate it like it was the greatest thing in the world. Right after he left I tried a piece. It was repulsive.

Scotty went back to his normal life and I went back to mine. I was sad I didn't have any pictures of him to show people who would never get a chance to see him, like Michele. One day I was in a Verizon store and noticed that he was on the brochure. A little something left over from his modeling days. I took about twenty and mailed them out to girlfriends with a little note that said, "Yep. I hit that." I also kept one for myself.

I was still panicked about my upcoming birthday, and it was starting to get me down. When you aren't feeling great about yourself, you make poor choices in men. I have definitely made some poor choices even when feeling good about myself, but the ones I made the last couple of years of my twenties were certainly the worst.

Jackie had left Mirabelle before me. In between us getting other jobs, we had a brief stint working together at another bar. The owner was the best. He was one of the funniest people I'd ever met. He could make me laugh like nobody else, which is probably why I was crazy about him. We became pretty close friends. And we all know how good I am at not falling for a close friend.

I can't say for sure that Patrick had a drinking problem, but I can say for sure that he used to mix vodka with Pedialyte so that he would automatically rehydrate as he got drunk. Bad sign? Maybe. Genius? Definitely.

I didn't date Patrick when I worked at his bar. I loved hanging out with him, but he had an intense love for strip bars and the girls who worked in them. He later claimed that he liked me then but had a strict rule about not dating employees. That may have been true, but if I had been an employee who also gave lap dances, my guess is he would have made an exception.

A few weeks after I quit working for him, we went out for drinks. Since I was no longer his employee, we had sex that night—or something similar to sex. We were both pretty drunk. I was now feeling very much like I wanted a boyfriend, and since he was in absolutely no place or condition to offer me that, I tried to make it happen.

Patrick and I always had a blast together. For the most part, we just got drunk, stayed up late singing country songs to each other, and repeatedly watched our mutual favorite movie, *Arthur*. If you think I'm talking about the Russell Brand remake, shame on you.

I can't call what we had a "relationship." I guess it wasn't much different than it was with Nico. If I tried to move it toward anything else, it didn't take. One day I realized we had never even been on a date. So I suggested that we go have a nice day at the beach, maybe even stay for a romantic dinner, like a real couple might do. He told me we could just get Bloody Marys, he'd throw celery salt at me, and that I could pretend it was sand. It made me laugh, but it also left me feeling pretty shitty. I pretended to be fine with where we were and what we were doing, but I wasn't. I was falling for him.

Patick had a dog that was really, really mean. Anytime he had company she had to be put in another room so that she wouldn't attack. Apparently she wasn't always like that, but as she got older she got bitter, just like a human.

One night at his apartment, he was in bed and I was up

watching SoapNet, which I couldn't afford to have at my own place. Once *General Hospital* ended, I decided to go to bed. I stripped down, thinking it would be a real turn-on to Patrick if I sauntered into his bedroom fully nude and ready for action. As usual when at his place, I wasn't completely sober. Unfortunately I forgot to knock first so that he could put his dog in the bathroom. The second I opened the door, I heard a loud growl and the sound of angry paws rushing me. Then I felt myself being knocked down to the ground. A few seconds later, the lights came on and the dog was nowhere in sight.

"She's in the bathroom. I have quick reflexes," Patrick explained.

Apparently when he heard the growl he shot out of bed and grabbed the dog. In the process he had also hip-checked me to the ground in order to save me. I looked up at him, naked, drunk, and in a ball on the floor. *At least I'm not wearing a choker.*

"I was trying to be sexy. Did it work?"

He laughed, scooped me up, and we went to sleep.

I don't know if the naked humiliation, the fact that I couldn't get along with his dog, or the fact that I could tell I was on my way to getting my heart ripped out was the tipping point, but things fizzled out between us. His lack of reaction to me not coming around anymore pretty much sealed my suspicion that I made the right call. I continued to carry a torch for a while, but that's nothing out of the ordinary.

For a few months after that I dated a guy who had a teenage son. He lived with the mother of his child but they were *just friends*. He explained it was best for the son that they all three live together. I'm sure that probably *is* best for a kid if you're hoping he'll one day rack up a huge bill with a therapist.

Adam was nice. He seemed to have a good job and some stability, if I didn't count his living situation. He was running some construction company and had the biceps to go with it. I liked the idea of being with someone who was not at all trying to be in the entertainment industry. A construction guy with a grown child was about as far off the mark of who I had dated in the past as I could get.

Adam had a steel plate in his mouth but I never really got the story as to why. He told me a couple of times, but it was so long and boring that I tuned out halfway through and just said things like "ouch, sounds awful" to give the illusion that I gave a shit. Unfortunately, as we dated, his real state of living started to reveal itself. The economy was taking its toll on his company. He always stayed at my apartment since I didn't want to stay at his house with his fucked-up family. He snored like an animal, which he said had something to do with the steel plate. He was impossible to wake up. Once while I was in Vegas working on the hidden-camera show, he fell asleep on my couch, directly on the remote control. He somehow managed to get his head to lay perfectly on the volume button and my TV went up so loud that my neighbor had to go into the basement and turn off the electricity to my entire apartment building so that she could get a decent night's sleep.

One day Adam suggested that we take his son to Magic Mountain. I tried everything I could think of to get out of it. I had my period, I felt a cold coming on, I shouldn't get on a roller coaster in case I was pregnant. Nothing got me out of it; it's not easy to win an argument with a man who lives every day sporting a metal jaw. I reluctantly agreed to the amusement park but forced my friend Casey to come with me. Her nephew was visiting her from out of town, and I figured two teenagers were better than one. I was wrong.

I hadn't met Adam's son yet so I tried to be open to the whole thing. I was pretty sure the relationship was going nowhere, but for some reason I still thought I needed to give it more effort. I was glad I had dragged Casey with me, but now I was with two teenagers at Magic Mountain. Did I mention it was July? I don't know if it was the heat or just the reality of the situation, but it was extremely unpleasant. I don't even like amusement parks in the first place. And I really don't like teenagers. (Note to my nephew, Nicholas: I'm not talking about you. I like you.) That day pretty much sealed the fate of my relationship with Adam, along with my desire to ever procreate.

Single again, I decided to touch base with Tilley. I hadn't seen her much over the last year or so and I decided that I should fix that. She was also about to turn thirty. I hadn't ever been on a real vacation, and now was the time. I called her and we plotted a getaway to Cancún.

We stayed at a resort, one of those that give you brace-lets and tell you to go nuts on the alcoholic beverages. I've never been fooled by those places—they don't put enough booze in the drinks and you just end up tired and bloated from the overconsumption of blended fruit. I warned Tilley of the scam so we stocked our room with real alcohol. I started to wonder if my Cancún trip was going to mirror my Cabo trip, which in some ways worried me. In other ways, like how I might get to fuck a hot guy with an accent, it made me hopeful.

For the most part, we lay around in hammocks all day and went to bars at night. It was fun, relaxing, and it got my mind off turning thirty, until one day when we went to rent a car and one of the guys working there asked if Tilley was my daughter. I wondered if Shirley's plastic surgery suggestion was something I should start to consider.

The final morning of our trip I woke up to the sound of the hotel phone ringing. Eyes still closed, I reached for it and put it to my ear.

"Hello?"

"Sarah?"

"Uh-huh. Who is this?"

"Ees Paco," the voice said.

"Paco?" Tilley heard me and shot up straight in bed.

"Oh, hold on," I said. "Must be the other Sarah."

I started to hand Tilley the phone and she shook her head. "Nope. That's for you."

Confused, I listened as Paco rambled on about how it was nice to meet me and maybe he'd be able to catch up with me in L.A. "Maybe I visit soon and I has you cellphone number. Talk to you later!"

I hung up and looked at Tilley. "He has my cellphone number?"

"He does," she said. "But don't look at me. You gave it to him."

"I did?" Why didn't I remember this? I mean, I knew I had a knack for meeting guys on vacation but this was embarrassing.

Then a sudden memory flashed through my mind. "Oh . . . Paco . . ."

Paco had been cleaning off the tables at the last bar we were hanging out in (that's my subtle way of saying that he was a busboy). I decided that he was cute and that busboys probably didn't get enough attention, so I flirted with him and gave him my phone number—hotel and cell, just to cover all the bases. I also tipped him everything that I had in my wallet when I told him about the car rental incident and he said there was *no way* I looked old enough to be Tilley's mom. He called me for about six months after that. I could hear the sounds of cars behind him and knew that he was calling from a pay phone. After a few attempts at talking I decided that when I saw an "unknown" number pop up I should always let it go to voice mail. I know I'm a good time, but the only reason a guy would be that persistent after meeting me for one night and not even having gotten sex out of it was that he needed a green card. I wasn't that desperate yet.

When I got back home I decided that I needed to have another mini-vacation for my thirtieth birthday. *Why not keep the ball rolling.* Joanna had also just turned thirty. She owned an apartment in New York that she rented out. Her tenants would be gone for the holidays and she thought it would be great if we spent my actual birthday there.

Joanna didn't mention to me that her apartment was the size of a litter box. I never knew what people were talking about when they said that the apartments in New York were tiny until I saw her place. The living room was the bedroom and the bedroom was the closet. The bathroom was so small that my knees stuck out of the door when I sat on the toilet and the kitchen was just big enough to turn on the stove and gas yourself to death in.

Her tenants left us a note that they had changed the sheets in the bunk beds and for us to make ourselves comfortable. Since that wasn't really possible, I took the bottom bunk.

Like me, Joanna is a big baseball fan. She loves the Yankees almost as much as she loved her dog Stevie, who had passed away just prior to our visit to the city. She had had him cremated and we decided that during our trip to New York we would take him to the Yankee Stadium tour and spread him on the field. Since this was probably frowned upon, we divided Stevie up and snuck him in—in ziplock bags. I'd never been to Yankee Stadium so I thought the whole tour was great. Joanna reminded me that we were there for a purpose, and that I needed to focus.

When they took us into the dugouts and we sat on the players' benches, I discreetly wriggled my bag of Stevie out of my coat pocket. I got it into the palm of my hand and began trying to unzip the bag. It was freezing and I was wearing gloves. I pulled a little too hard and ripped the bag open, which made the ashes sail all over the place, including onto the coat of the woman sitting next to me. She was paying too much attention to what our tour guide was saying to realize that I had just gotten cremated dog all over her, which I was grateful for. I cleared my throat until Joanna looked up and made eye contact with me. I nodded my head in the direction of the woman's ashy coat and made an "I'm so sorry face." She couldn't quite tell what I was trying to say, so I whispered to her:

"Stevie's on that lady's coat."

I patiently waited, dreading her reaction.

Joanna took a minute to process what I said, but eventually put it together. Her eyes welled up with tears. I thought she was going to lose it. She started laughing. "Hopefully she's visiting from Europe," Joanna replied. "Stevie always wanted to see Paris."

Chelsea was also in New York that week, performing at Caroline's Comedy Club, so Joanna and I decided to go see her on the night of my birthday. The show was really fun but I was still feeling restless. I was nervous that I was thirty and I wasn't sure how to shake it.

We all went out after the show, and ran into some other comics whom Chelsea seemed to know. One was kind of cute. Actually he wasn't, but I was drunk and he was flirting with me.

He told me that his name was Ryan. That reminded me that I was supposed to try to meet up with another guy named Ryan while I was in New York. I had met him in L.A. when he came in to Formosa with some friends of mine. You'd think after Nico I'd be turned off from dating customers, but in case you haven't noticed, I always make the same mistakes at least twice. Ryan Friend of Friend had told me he was going to be in New York at the same time I was and thought maybe we could get together. I quickly went to the bathroom, texted him, then went back to the bar and flirted with Ryan Comic.

After several hours of drinking, I found myself sitting on a curb eating a huge slice of pizza while Joanna and Chelsea hailed a cab. When one finally pulled over, we all piled in the back then looked up to see that Ryan Comic had gotten in the front seat. Joanna and Chelsea looked at me. I shrugged and sighed, "It's my birthday." I had to make out with someone so unless one of them was up for the challenge, it looked like it was going to be Ryan Comic.

I had forgotten how small Joanna's place was until we got back and saw it through Chelsea's eyes. When we walked in, she looked around like she'd been taken hostage.

"Well, this is stupid," she said. "I'm sleeping on the top bunk since it's as far away from all of you as I can get." With that she hopped in bed.

Joanna crawled onto the bottom bunk, so Ryan Comic and I were left to tangle up on the world's smallest couch. We made out for about ten seconds before I decided that I wasn't interested in him and fake passed out. He tried to wake me, but luckily I'm so good at fake passing out that I wound up passing out.

When we all woke up the next morning, Ryan Comic was gone. I checked my phone to see if Ryan Friend of Friend had called me back but he hadn't. I felt a pang of disappointment. Chelsea and Joanna woke up and immediately started making fun of me for allowing Ryan Comic to come back with us.

"He was like thirty-eight," Chelsea said.

"Really?" Joanna asked. "I thought he was forty-eight. The bald spot must have mixed me up."

"Okay, okay, I get it," I conceded. "But at least I didn't do anything with him. And it could have been worse; I could have brought back the German wrestler we met at that one bar."

"Good point," Chelsea added. "Weren't you supposed to leave at nine for your flight?"

"Yes," I said. "What time is it?"

"Nine forty-five."

I was flying out of Long Island and had completely missed the train I was supposed to take. There was barely enough time to make it, but if I took a cab I might be fine. Chelsea had to lend me a hundred dollars in order to get me to the airport. I was really starting off my thirties on the right foot. I'm also pretty sure I never paid her back. Chelsea, if you're reading this, I owe you a hundred bucks.

When I got back to Los Angeles, I heard back from Ryan Friend of Friend. He said that he had been pretty busy while he was in New York and was sorry that we didn't get a chance to meet up. He wondered if I'd like to go see a movie or something. I said yes.

The first date I went on with Ryan Friend of Friend was the best first date I've ever been on. Nothing special happened; we saw *Ocean's Twelve* and went out to dinner. He scored points right off the bat by taking me to the movie first. I like it that way, because then you have something to talk about at dinner, although there isn't a ton to dissect in a George Clooney sequel. *He* probably just figured if we had dinner last, when he took me home I'd still have a buzz from the nice wine he ordered, and we could fool around. He was correct.

We went to this little French place in Hollywood that I love. It's got great food, a patio, and a good wine selection. When the bill came he opened it and said, "What the fuck did you have?" which made me laugh. I decided for that I'd let him touch my boobs.

Ryan really wasn't my "type." He always dressed like he was about to go on a hike, you know, like a lesbian. He loved to buy clothes at REI, which is where people shop when they are about to go on a camping trip or need bug spray for a weekend in Costa Rica. He also loved to talk about how the shirt he was wearing also repelled water or how his shoes could be worn in a lake.

"Well, are you going to a lake?" I'd ask.

"No."

"Then why can't you just wear land shoes?"

Regardless, it was crazy to me how much I wanted to hump him.

That hadn't been the case when we'd first met. He'd come up to me when I was working one night to tell me that he'd been in the bar a few months before and I'd given him back the wrong credit card at the end of the night. Apparently it made a trip to Vegas a real hassle for him and he wanted to tell me all about it.

"So a few months ago I mixed up your credit card and you came in here on a Saturday night at eleven P.M. to let me know?" I asked. I was really busy, and really annoyed.

"I play softball with Mike Gould. He told me you'd think it was funny. I was mad about it all this time, but he insisted that you're really cool. So I thought I'd just—"

"Sorry about your credit card. Can I get back to work now?" I walked off. *Who is this dick?*

He came back up to me later to try to explain again his motivation for telling me his story. "Hey, I wasn't trying to bother you earlier when I told you that story. I just thought—"

"It's not personal. I'm just really busy."

"Okay, good. So it's your problem," he snapped. Then he walked away.

I told Mike later that night how annoying his friend was. He laughed. "He said the same thing about you."

A few weeks later Ryan came back into the bar, and I wasn't as busy. I was talking to some other customers and he overheard that I did stand-up. Then he realized he'd seen me perform before.

"You're really funny. I saw you at the Improv a couple of months ago. I just put it together that it was you," he told me.

That's when I softened on him. After all, he thought I was funny.

# THE CUSTOMER IS NEVER RIGHT

**U**nfortunately, even though Ryan and I had had a great first date, it became really obvious that he was still hung up on his ex-girlfriend. I was 75 percent sure that she was a lesbian, and I figured that since he dressed like one maybe they were meant for each other and I shouldn't get in the middle. Either way, it was clear he was involved in an on-again, off-again relationship that always seemed like it was about to be on-again.

I was visiting my dad in Palm Desert, where he'd moved so that he could play golf on a regular basis. We went out to dinner and after five drinks I ended up telling him about Ryan.

"Sounds like a good guy," my dad told me.

Given my dad's track record, I made the decision to break

things off with Ryan the next day. I called him on my drive home and told him we could just be friends.

"It's obvious you and Mary are still talking, and I don't really have an interest in dating you while you try to figure that out," I told him flatly.

"I understand. This is sad, though, Sarah. I really like you."

"It's not sad. It would have been sad later, but I stopped it before it could get sad," I told him calmly while I repeatedly blinked in order to stop the tears from flowing. "I have to go, the freeway is a mess." I hung up and coasted home. I'd never seen the freeway so empty before.

Ryan and I became really good friends after that. I still had a huge crush on him and hanging out with him only made it worse, so I did it on a regular basis. Obviously I'd learned nothing from Andy, Patrick, and the list goes on. I continued to break my own rule of not hanging out with an ex. Since these guys were friends first, I had found a loophole.

When Ryan got back together with his ex for a while, I retaliated by dating a customer I met at Formosa. I *know*.

The first night I met him, Gavin was cryptic about what he did for a living. I was bartending and he was drinking—so I wrote down the name on his credit card and went home and Googled him. I quickly figured out why he wouldn't tell me what he did for a living. Not all porn editors are proud of their jobs.

The next time that he came in I told him I knew what he did. He was definitely pursuing me and I needed to let him know that while my standards might not be high, they were higher than porn.

He explained that it was just a way to make money. He

wanted to act and he wanted to edit real movies, he said, but for now editing pornography was paying the bills. He made it seem like it wasn't a big deal. I decided to lower my standards. I needed someone to date so that I could show Ryan that I was *so* not interested in *him*. I *know*.

Gavin didn't have his own place. He lived with an old man who used to be an acting teacher, or something like that. He said the old man needed help from time to time and he offered to let Gavin live in his house rent-free if Gavin could lend him a hand. So far Gavin was turning out to be a real catch. I opted to stick it out and just not tell Ryan any of those details.

I stayed the night at his house one time after we started seeing each other. It was creepy and musty and old, just like the acting teacher. He was certainly making enough money to get a small, shitty apartment, so clearly he was either really cheap or secretly involved in a twisted gay relationship with the old man.

He had two dogs and two cats and they all stayed in his bedroom with him. Apparently that was the only room that was really his. The fucking dogs were the size of grown men and they slept in his bed with him. His room was covered in Superman posters and dog hair. I still didn't run. I *know*.

The Superman obsession didn't stop with the poster. He had the giant *S* logo in the form of a sticker on his car. He also had a Superman tattoo. I guess I was dating a Super Loser.

Unfortunately *Superman Returns* came out while we were dating. I had never seen a Superman movie and I had hoped to keep it that way. Gavin, on the other hand, behaved in the days leading up to the release of that movie as if Jesus were about to pay him a visit. He even pulled one of those really annoying moves and got tickets to the first showing at midnight the day it opened.

"I waited in line for five hours for these," he said, beaming.

"That's great," I lied. Then I called Jackie and asked her if that was normal behavior for a man in his thirties.

"No, it isn't," she scolded me. "He's ridiculous. Why are you still dating him?"

"Have you broken things off with that prick Colin yet?" I asked.

"No."

"When you stop seeing him, I'll stop seeing Gavin."

"God, maybe I should move back onto your couch. At least then we were having some fun."

I bought four airplane-size bottles of vodka and met Gavin at the movie theater.

"You want anything from the concession?" he asked. "We should get it now and go get a seat right up front."

Up front at a movie? Worse—at a *Superman* movie. We really had nothing in common. "I just want lemonade," I told him. "But only fill it up halfway." It was going to be a long two hours.

The movie was horrible, and to make matters worse it was in 3-D. Twenty minutes in, I had already finished all of the alcohol I had with me and was trying to figure out if there was something in the seat that I could kill myself with. I looked over at Gavin. He was grinning from ear to ear. I don't think I'd ever seen anybody look so happy. *Oh my God, he's retarded.*

I broke things off with Gavin two days after the movie. I would have done it the next day, but I was so annoyed about the movie that I couldn't even talk to him long enough to break up with him.

I decided to invite him to lunch and told him I thought we were going "in different directions." He got really upset, which I wasn't expecting.

"Is it because of the porn thing?" he asked. "I want to get out of it. It's just that right now it pays the bills."

"It's not that. It should be, but it's not."

"I don't believe you. It ruined things with my ex-wife and now it's ruining things with you."

"Your ex-what?"

"Didn't I tell you I was married?"

"No, you didn't." *It wouldn't have mattered if you did. If that whole acting teacher/animal situation didn't run me off I doubt an ex-wife would have.*

"Well, I was married. For almost three years."

"And she didn't like that you edited adult movies for a living?"

"She didn't care about that. But she was in some of them, so it just got weird when I'd have to cut her scenes with some other dude."

I stopped chewing my turkey burger. I looked for a place to spit it out. I couldn't find one. I swallowed. I assumed his ex-wife did, too.

"Your ex-wife was in porn? She was a porn star? She had sex with people on camera and you watched?"

He didn't really say much after that, other than "yes" when I demanded to know if he'd been tested for HIV.

"Well, this has been great. I came here to break up with you, so I'm going to stick to that and get on out of here. You can go ahead and pay the bill. Don't forget to leave a nice tip."

Much like Nico, Gavin lived within walking distance of Formosa. He continued to come into the bar and have drinks long after we quit seeing each other. *I really need to get a new job.*

## MOVE IT OR LOSE IT

Ryan and I continued to be friends throughout it all. Every time I dated someone, I couldn't wait to tell Ryan about it in hope of a reaction. If that sounds familiar, go back a few chapters. It is.

All of Ryan's friends hated Mary, which was very satisfying, especially since they all liked me. They continued to break up and get back together like a couple of dumb high school kids, while I continued to harbor secret feelings for him. She and I never met. I don't know why she was fine with her boyfriend constantly going to movies and dinners with some girl she didn't know, but she was. Or she didn't know anything about it. I didn't really ask. I just knew that they led very separate lives for a couple. I was positive that there was no way they could last, which kept me from developing anything real with anybody else. In case it isn't obvious, I really, really liked Ryan.

Ryan was really successful in voice-over and made a pretty good living. Mary had a pretty great voice-over career, too, so I decided that was why he liked her better. *Why would he want to be with a bartender?*

My own lack of career stability made me feel really insecure and inferior, even though he seemed pretty impressed with my dedication to pursuing what I loved. It's weird when other people are comfortable with your life and you aren't. Then again, they aren't balancing your sad checking account at 3 A.M. while polishing off a bottle of cheap cabernet.

Eventually Ryan and Mary ended things for good. She didn't leave him for a woman as I had predicted, but she did end up lying to him and proving that she was an asshole. They'd taken a sort of "trial separation" but she kept telling Ryan she wanted to work things out. In the meantime, she had a full-on other boyfriend. He finally decided that he deserved better: me.

Ryan and I went out for drinks a couple of nights after they broke things off. I was happy to be there for him. At the end of the night, he tried to kiss me. It really, really pissed me off.

"I'm not a fucking backup plan," I told him.

"You aren't, it's just that now I'm finally done with that relationship and would like to try one with you."

"You've had about forty-eight hours to get over it. Let's give it more time."

My brave front crumbled quickly and before I knew it Ryan and I were in a relationship. He and Mary had only been broken up for a few weeks, but here we were. It felt good, and we had fun when we were together, but I couldn't shake the feeling that I was a consolation prize for what he'd just lost.

He didn't do a ton to help his plight. As we dated, I started to realize why his ex-girlfriend and I had never met. He was really secretive, and not even about things that people need to be secretive about. If I wanted to know what he bought at Banana Republic that day I was being "pushy." If I wondered who he was texting I was being "insecure." That one might have actually been accurate. But give me a break. We didn't exactly start strong. In his defense, I'm pretty nosy. I guess I need someone who can deal with it.

Ryan liked to go home to Philly as often as he could to visit his family. If he didn't invite me, I'd invite myself. I was really trying to get this relationship to the next level. I began to realize that someone had a real issue with commitment and for once it wasn't me. In fact, I was so busy trying to show him he had nothing to be afraid of that I had forgotten about my own fears.

I stayed the night with Ryan all the time, but he rarely stayed the night with me. He had a roommate and I lived alone, so you'd think it would have been the other way around. I didn't understand what the problem was. Over the course of a few months, I realized that the reason he preferred to stay at his place was that it was his place. It was easier for him. He was comfortable. He didn't like change. That was going to be a problem.

"God, Ryan. I don't even have a place to put stuff. It's a huge pain for me to go back and forth. I'm a girl. I need my shit and this place doesn't have any of it."

Most guys would just have started staying at my place to shut me up, but he was incredibly stubborn. Any move toward compromise was just me being even pushier and him losing in his imaginary battle.

That's why he was very excited to announce to me one day that he had solved our problem. He had cleaned out a drawer in his dresser, and I was free to do with it what I would.

"A drawer?" I asked, hoping I'd heard him wrong.

"Yeah! A drawer! Now it won't be such a pain to come back and forth here. You'll have a place to put stuff."

He was really trying, but he was definitely missing the point. I took the drawer. I put stuff in it. I tried to take the baby steps with him. Unfortunately, I'm a really fast walker.

After we'd been together for more than two years it was clear that he had no interest in living with me. We had a long conversation. I told him that I wanted to get married someday and that if he couldn't even stomach living with me after all this time, that was certainly never going to happen. He was five years older than me and I figured if a man in his late thirties preferred to have a roommate over me, I wasn't the girl for him.

Ryan didn't see it that way. He was of the mindset that moving in was something that "just happened" and that me suggesting we do it was him being pushed again.

"Moving in can't really 'just happen,' Ryan. There are apartment hunting and movers and all kinds of things that have to take place, which involve decision-making and talking. And you can't keep waiting for your fears to subside. You have to fucking try."

It didn't matter what I said; he wouldn't budge. I couldn't believe that I was the one trying to convince someone that moving in together was no big deal. At least he had a roommate; I'd been living alone for seven years and the thought of having to give up my alone time terrified me. But for the first time ever, my desire to find out what it could be like to take the next step was outweighing my insecurities. I wanted to take the risk and he didn't. We broke up. I was heart-broken.

I continued working hard on my career. *Audition, stand-up, make drinks for people, repeat.* I just needed to stay busy. I was in my early thirties and single once again. I told myself that it was okay, that I hadn't walked away from something great, that he didn't deserve me if he didn't want to try to move forward. The alcohol helped.

One of our good friends had a birthday party and both Ryan and I showed up. The problem was, it was a small party, about ten people, so it was totally uncomfortable for everybody that we were both there. The birthday honoree had been his friend first, so I didn't stay long. I had put a lot of work into looking good, knowing I would see him, so I just said I had another "event" to go to and got the fuck out of there. There was no event, just my couch. I stopped at the nearest liquor store, picked up a bottle of wine, went home, drank it, then joined eHarmony.

Two days later I got an email from eHarmony telling me that they'd found my perfect match. I hadn't really paid any attention to it since I drunkenly joined, but I was intrigued to see what they'd come up with.

"Ryan from Philly is your perfect match," my email read. I found it really annoying that they'd set me up with someone with the same name as my ex-boyfriend and from the same city as my ex-boyfriend. Still, I went to scope out my future husband's profile.

eHarmony didn't match me with a guy with the same

name as my ex-boyfriend. They matched me with my ex-boyfriend. It's possible that I've never been so angry in my entire life. I immediately called Ryan and went off.

"What the hell are you doing on eHarmony?" I asked him.

He was confused. He hadn't gotten the "Sarah from Arkansas is your perfect match" email yet.

"What are you talking about?"

"eHarmony just matched us up. You're 'Ryan from Philly.' You're my perfect match, you stupid, stupid jerk."

"Wait, I just joined that. Wait, they matched us up? Wait . . ."

"Yes, you dumb, dumb asshole. And guess what? You shouldn't fucking be on eHarmony. Have you seen the commercials? It's for people who want a relationship, people who want to get married and shit, it's not for people like you. It's not for people who can't give somebody more than a drawer. Did you put 'terrified of commitment' in the 'about me' section?"

Ryan was actually more freaked out than I was. "Well, what are *you* doing on eHarmony?"

"Uh, I am not the one with the commitment issues. I went on it to find a mature, healthy relationship. I never said I didn't want to be in one, so I'm not the big fat liar."

"I never said I didn't want to be in one, either, Sarah. I just said I didn't want to move in yet."

"Oh shut up. Just shut up with your bullshit. eHarmony is so stupid. And you're so stupid." I was handling this great for someone who had just accused the other person of not being mature.

We were both silent for what felt like ten minutes. I refused to speak until he apologized.

"I'm sorry Sarah. When I saw you at Sean's party, you looked so pretty. Like you were going on a date. Then you just left and never said a word to me. I stopped at a liquor store, then went home and drank. I got pretty banged up, then I went on the computer and joined eHarmony," he explained.

"That's the most pathetic story I've ever heard," I told him.

I hung up and called eHarmony customer care.

"Yes, I need to cancel my subscription," I told the customer service representative.

"Okay. I can cancel it now. It will disable one month from the date that you joined," the lady said oh so sweetly.

"That's not good enough. I need it completely canceled now. Also I need a refund."

"We don't do refunds."

"You set me up with my ex-boyfriend. I need a refund."

"I'm sorry, ma'am—"

"Don't call me ma'am. I'm sure you're older than me."

"I'm twenty-seven."

"Can you just get me a fucking refund, please?"

"Our computers match people based on interests and goals. If you and your ex are both on the site, we can't help the possibility that you might be matched up. Perhaps that's why you were together before—you had similar interests. So if you look at it from our point of view, we're doing a really good job."

"If you look at it from my point of view, this is the worst day ever. I filled out a whole bunch of shit and I made it very clear that I wanted to find someone who can handle an adult relationship. 'Ryan from Philly' is not capable of that. He's a commitment-phobe and you set me up with him on your site that's supposedly all about people who want a commitment. That's false advertising. I want my fucking fifty-four ninety-nine back." I was crying.

"Sorry, ma'am. We can't refund your money. But your account will cancel in one month. In the meantime, maybe you'll get matched with someone who—"

"Someone who will chop my head off?" I yelled. "For all I know I could be set up with a serial killer, because clearly you don't have a screening process." I hung up. Obviously she wasn't going to budge on the refund.

I met Casey for afternoon cocktails the next day in the middle of the old farmer's market. It was and still is one of my favorite drinking spots. Most of the patrons there are senior citizens and the ladies drink white zinfandel out of plastic wineglasses. It's always good people-watching. We definitely didn't go there to meet guys, since most of them were in their early nineties. But that afternoon we ended up talking to two men and I found one of them really, really cute. They didn't stay long, but later that night the one I was flirting with walked into Formosa. I had mentioned in passing that I worked there, and he decided to come in to ask me out. It was a pretty bold move. *Ryan who?*

Aidan and I went on a few dates. He worked at a studio building sets, so he was slightly in the entertainment industry but not really. He was more of a construction worker. I decided not to hold my past with construction workers against him.

Aidan had a nice house, a nice car, and a nine-year-old son. *What is it with guys who build things for a living not wearing protection?* I wondered.

Our relationship was very new and very casual, so luckily he never tried to get me to meet his kid. He just made me dinner and took me to sushi. It was the perfect distraction from what I was coming out of. And he was fun.

Just when I started to really like him, I ran into Ryan.

"You have the worst timing," I told him.

He didn't even ask what I meant. He just told me that he wanted to take me out for dinner.

"No thanks," I replied.

"What do you mean?"

"I mean no thanks I don't want to go out for dinner."

"Okay, smart-ass. But I want to take you out. I want to talk to you."

"Talk to me here," I insisted.

"We're in a parking lot."

"So, talk to me in a parking lot."

"Sarah, I would like to take you out and talk to you."

"I don't want to talk to you."

"You might want to hear what I have to say."

"Say it here."

I won't bore you with the rest of that conversation. If you guessed that it continued to go on like that for ten minutes and was really annoying, you guessed correctly. Eventually he broke me down and I accepted the invitation to go to dinner with him the next evening.

I got home from running into Ryan and started to get ready for a date I had with Aidan that night. It dawned on me that I had two dates in two nights. *This is what it must have felt like for Stella when she got her groove back,* I thought as I put on a pair of really uncomfortable heels.

While I was getting ready, I got a phone call from the Hollywood Improv asking if I could come do a set on the 10 P.M. show that night to fill in for someone who had canceled. I had to say yes, it was work, so I called Aidan to ask if we could reschedule our date.

"I'm so sorry, but they just called me," I explained to him. "I should definitely show up." I probably should have invited him to come, but I don't like for guys to see me perform too early on in the relationship. It's better for them to find out that I'm kind of slutty on their own time.

"All right, fine. Have fun," he responded.

"Thanks. Do you want to try to get together maybe over the weekend?"

No response.

"Hello?" All I heard was silence. I assumed that the call had dropped. I tried him back and he didn't pick up. Nor did he try to call me back.

Later, on my way home from the Improv, I got a text from him that said, "Sorry, but I'm looking for someone with a little more care." *Oh my God, really?* This guy was in his late forties. I didn't want to be with a guy who got his period. Aidan was also a big pot smoker, which I'm not a huge fan of. It's okay in increments, but when someone does it too much they become the "what's the rush, we have all the time in the world!" kind of guy. Sometimes you don't have all the time in the world. Sometimes the movie starts at eight. Since I had a date with Ryan the next night, I figured this was just the universe working it all out for me anyway. Aidan did later try to retract his childish attitude, but I had already shifted my focus back to Ryan.

The next day I got home from the gym (that's my way of telling you that sometimes I work out) and found a bag on my porch. I picked it up, then spotted my neighbor. "Did you happen to see who left this here?" I asked her.

"No, sorry. Hope you had a nice swim." She went inside. *Swim?* I had no idea what was she talking about.

Then I looked down at my clothes and noticed how sweaty they were. *Great, I sweat so much that she thinks it's from swimming. Worse, she thinks I swim in workout clothes.*

When I got inside and opened the bag, I found a really pretty black dress. It was from BCBG, which was where Ryan always bought my Christmas presents. I immediately called my mom, who'd been there for me over the weeks following our breakup.

"Ryan bought me a dress. He left it on my doorstep. Should I wear it tonight or is that too *Pretty Woman?*"

"Don't wear it, and don't go to dinner."

"What? I thought you'd think it was great that he wanted to go to dinner. He probably wants to get back together," I told her. "Shouldn't I hear what he has to say? And the dress probably cost like a hundred and fifty dollars."

"Of course he wants to get back together," she assured me. "But you broke up with him for a reason. Don't go out with him and listen to his crap unless he gives you a ring."

"A ring?" *Slow down, Mom.* I did think I wanted to marry Ryan, but not quite yet.

"*Yes.* A ring. He's been getting the milk for free for months and now it's time to buy the cow."

"And I'm the cow?"

"Oh hush. You know what I mean."

"I just want to move in together for now. I don't think I'm ready for a ring yet. We have to find out if we can live under the same roof."

"As your mother, I'd like to say that that is backwards, and that you're supposed to live together *after* you get married. But as your friend, I'm going to say that it isn't a bad idea to do a test run."

"Thanks, Mom. I am going to meet him. But . . . I won't wear the dress. I'll let you know what happens." I felt I had made a good compromise. Obviously when it came to Ryan, I had my weaknesses.

At dinner, Ryan kept trying to make small talk. I wasn't having it.

"Tell me why we're here," I said flatly. I was holding on to my brave front as best I could.

"Okay. No time for catch-up, I guess?"

"No, I don't want to sit through an entire meal, especially since I know how much we both love appetizers, only to find out you just wanted to know what I've been up to."

Ryan ended up saying what I wanted to hear. He said that he'd missed me, that he'd done a lot of thinking, and that he was ready to move forward. He told me how scared he was.

"So am I, Ryan. I've never lived with someone I was dating, either. In fact, I've lived alone a long time now. The thought of having to share my space with someone else, to have to watch a show on TV that I don't want to watch . . . the thought of someone else eating the leftover pizza that I was counting on having for breakfast the next day. It all pisses me off to even think about."

"Then why are you so dead set on doing it?" he asked.

"Because I'm finally willing to figure out if the good can outweigh that fear."

"So am I. That's why we're here," he responded. We finished our meal, went to his place and had sex, and then I made him take me home.

I didn't talk the whole ride back to my place. I was afraid I'd screwed up. That I was caving in too soon. I was afraid he wasn't going to follow through.

He called me the next afternoon. "You just have sex with a guy and don't call the next day?" he tried to joke.

"You're the man. You're supposed to call." I read that in a book in the early nineties.

He laughed. I didn't. I was mad at him for taking me to his place. I was mad at myself for going. I wondered why he didn't drive me home and come in and spend the night with me. That had been such a sticking point in the past. That move would have been a nice way to show me he was serious about the future, and that he was listening.

"Okay, Sarah. I know you are skeptical. But don't be. I meant everything that I said."

The next week we started looking for apartments, which took a couple of months. If he didn't like a place, I worried that it was just his way of stalling things, but I could tell he was at least trying. It was a step in the right direction, or so I thought.

## ALONE TIME

**D**uring the prior year, Chelsea had gotten her own show. Our lives had gone off in different directions. We were still friends, we just didn't see each other as much as we used to. A few months into it she'd invited me to come and do what comics did on the show, which was the roundtable. It went really well so they continued to have me on. It was a lot of fun to be sitting next to my friend of twelve years while she hosted her own show.

One afternoon Ryan and I had an appointment to look at a place that we were both really excited about. I was going to meet him there straight from shooting an episode of *Chelsea Lately*. The executive producer asked me to stick around after the show, and he and Chelsea offered me a full-time writing job. They told me to think about it for a couple of days, so I pretended to. *I'm going to set my black bar-tending pants on fire,* I thought as I drove to meet Ryan. Then I remembered how long it took with those fucking jeans Jackie made me burn and decided maybe I would just give them to Goodwill.

It felt like the job came out of nowhere, but I guess it didn't. It's just how it works. You keep going, trying, getting jobs here and there and then finally one day you get the job that changes everything. I suppose it's the same way with dating.

When I got to the apartment, I told Ryan about the offer. We were both so excited. Then we went in to look at the apartment and we both loved it. I couldn't believe all of this was happening at the same time.

When the time came for us to move in, I said goodbye to the apartment I'd lived in for almost eight years, only weeks after saying goodbye to the bar I had worked in for seven. Everything was finally coming together.

The first night in our new place I cooked dinner. We ate really dry chicken and watched TV. The next morning I got up and went to work, leaving extra early since I hadn't yet timed my morning commute from the new place. I had my Sirius radio tuned in to Howard Stern and thought about what an adult I was now. For the first time since I moved away, I couldn't wait to go home for Christmas and run into someone from high school.

I drove home that night, wondering what had happened on *General Hospital.* I was ready for my glass of wine and TiVo when I walked in the door about an hour later. I threw my purse down and went upstairs to settle in. There was Ryan, on the couch, watching *SportsCenter.*

"Hey," he said, smiling. "How was your day?"

I stared at him. *Oh great,* I thought. *I was really hoping to have some time to myself.*

It turns out that I'm not very good at sharing a place with someone else. I don't know if it's from fear, or from years of living alone, or if I'm just an asshole. Maybe it's all three.

For the almost two years that we lived together, we definitely had some fun. Ryan's a great cook, and I'm a great eater. We had our favorite local spots for dinner, coffee, drinks. We had people over to watch our favorite show, *24,* on Monday nights. We were playing the parts we thought we were supposed to be playing. And I knew that I loved him, so why wasn't it working?

I'm not sure what shifted, but something did. I became really busy with work. Between the show and the new, improved world of stand-up gigs it was opening me up to, I wasn't home very often. I worked all day, then went away on the weekends to perform. And when I was available, I wasn't really available to him. I was loving what I was doing, but in turn I wasn't spending the time I needed to spend with my partner. It wasn't fair. But I also felt he didn't like me anymore. He loved me, but I didn't feel like he liked me. I was growing comfortable in my own skin, finally okay with who I had and have become. I wanted him to like who I was now. Yet I could feel him judging me for allowing myself to finally be me. *Here I go again.* We were growing apart.

It was really confusing for me to consider that I might not want to be with the man I wanted to be with for so long. I couldn't tell if that was a real feeling or if I was just tired of the push and pull. I threatened to move out a couple of times, not even sure if I wanted to or what I wanted his reaction to be. It was just clear that a square peg was trying to fit into a round hole. And I used to really love his peg.

I found myself filling my free time with plans that didn't involve him. My career was finally fulfilling and I was focused on keeping that going, so in turn maybe I was losing focus on my relationship. I'm sure there's a way to balance it. There has to be—people do it all the time. Maybe I haven't found the balance, or maybe I just hadn't found the right person to balance with me.

After all of the heartache and the pushing, we finally decided to part ways. We were both heartbroken. We were both losing our best friends.

"We tried," I reminded him over and over. "We really tried."

I was so afraid he was going to yell at me for making him move in with me in the first place. I probably would have, had the situation been reversed. But he didn't. He's more mature than me. I do believe we had to take that step. We could have kept on the way that we were going, creeping along, and eventually I'd have been getting my Depends out of my pathetic little "drawer" and taking out my teeth in his roommate's bathroom. We did the right thing; it just didn't work.

It's a funny feeling when you break up with someone in your thirties. In my twenties, the reaction was always to go have sex with someone else. *That will fix it.* It never did. I mean it was fun, but it didn't fix anything.

Now, in my thirties, once Ryan and I broke up, the last thing on my mind was touching another man. The thought made me physically ill. It felt like cheating. For quite some time I had only let Ryan touch me that way, and I didn't want to betray that.

A few months later, something woke up. My vagina reminded me that it was still there, and that it didn't want to be ignored. The weight of what Ryan and I carried was lifting. It still hurt, but it was lifting.

Now I'm just trying to figure out the next step and I'm wondering what it will be like to date again after four years. Clearly I'm not going to join eHarmony again. I'm still pissed off about those assholes not giving me a refund.

# CLOSING ARGUMENT

So I'm sitting alone in that same apartment that I once shared with Ryan. I have a big glass of vodka next to me. I've filled it four times so far and it's 8 P.M. I've only been home since six. Whatever, it's Monday.

I'm trying to figure out how to finish this book. I've ended it, but I haven't finished it. I suppose that's what I did with Ryan. With Ira. Not really with Lo-Waisted, since he was finished before he started. But it's always easier to end something than it is to finish it. You can end a relationship, but sometimes it's still awhile before you're really finished with it.

I'm still really busy with work. But I love it. To finally be able to say all of my career dreams are coming true feels pretty great. I work my ass off, then I go on fun trips and travel more than I ever thought that I would.

I feel like I've found my balance. I know how to enjoy my cocktails at the times that I have the freedom to do so. And how to work when I need to work. I don't know if I'll be able to balance my life with the next guy, or the guy after that, or the guy after that. Or maybe there's just going to be one more guy and he'll be the one who tips the scales in just the right direction. I don't blame Ryan, or anyone else that things didn't work out with. I'm just glad to know that I'm finally comfortable with the two personalities living inside me. They get along pretty well. I don't have to keep them apart or hide them from their separate groups of friends. And now I just have to find the guy who loves them both, too.

So I'm open to finding someone new. I don't know if it's for sex, love, or both. I just know I'm open to it. I'm not pushing for it. What happens next happens next. I'd like to say that now that I've grown up, have my career in place, and like who I am, I'm going to handle being single with class. But I'm still capable of repeating mistakes, so I don't want to end this with a lie. I just know that I'm excited and intrigued to find out what's next.

Hopefully, I won't blow it.

# ACKNOWLEDGMENTS

I want to thank and acknowledge the following people:

Both of my sets of parents, Eric and Cheryl Henderson and Jim and Shirley Colonna, for always believing in me, and for the bonus Christmas presents one gets when one's parents are divorced.

Jennifer Colonna-Quinton for being the best big sister I could ask for.

Chelsea Handler, for more reasons than I have room to list. I love you, girl.

My book agent, Robert Guinsler, whom I had never met before but who wrote me an email and said, "Why haven't you written a book?" You made me do this—so this is your fault.

My editor Ryan Doherty, who not only gave me amazing notes and ideas, but didn't judge me for the stories in this book—at least not out loud.

Jane von Mehren from Random House, for believing in this in the first place.

Chris Franjola, Jen Kirkman, Tom Brunelle, Sue Murphy, Dan Maurio, Heather McDonald, Brad Wollack, Jeff Wild, Josh Wolf, Steve Marmalstein, and Fortune Feimster. Thanks for loving me even when I'm acting like a bitch, and for making me laugh every day.

Everyone else at *Chelsea Lately*. You are all so important to me, individually and as a group.

Joe Mortimer, for putting up with me while I wrote this. And for much, much more.

Gina Wachtel, Beth Pearson, Ashley Gratz-Collier, Greg Mortimer, Leigh Merchant, Kelli Fillingim, and everyone at Random House for the work they contributed to this book.

The people who have believed in and continue to believe in my career and fight for it: Abbey MacDonald (all ninety pounds of her), Michael Pelmont, Lindsay Howard, Melissa Orton, Tim Scally, Joe Schwartz, Dan Baron, and everybody else at APA and New Wave. And Jeff Cohen and Cynthia Sohl, for standing behind me even when I was only able to pay them back by serving them cocktails.

Todd Gallopo and Zan Passante, for the amazing work they did on the cover. Who knew a photo shoot could be fun?

Amy Meyer, Gina Monaci, and Michele Bottarini, for making me look pretty for said shoot.

Lisa Perkins and Alex Martinetti.

All of my friends—you know who you are—thank you.

I love you and you've made my life better by being a part of it.

All of the Morgans and Colonnas, for being my family, supporting me, and providing me with a wealth of material.

Finally, my nephew, Nicholas, for not ratting me out to my sister every time I drop the F-bomb.

## ABOUT THE AUTHOR

SARAH COLONNA is a writer and roundtable regular on the hit late-night talk show *Chelsea Lately*, and a producer and star of *After Lately*. She has been performing stand-up in Los Angeles and across the country for several years and has appeared on various television shows. She used to drink bourbon, but now prefers vodka.